M000278348

RAISED BED GARDENING COMPILATION FOR BEGINNERS AND EXPERIENCED GARDENERS

THE ULTIMATE GUIDE TO PRODUCE ORGANIC VEGETABLES WITH TIPS TO INCREASE YOUR GROWING SUCCESS

PETER SHEPPERD

For Carmen; for being herself.

CONTENTS

INTRODUCTION TO RAISED BED GARDENING

ADVANCED RAISED BED GARDENING GUIDE

INTRODUCTION TO RAISED BED GARDENING

THE ULTIMATE BEGINNER'S GUIDE TO STARTING A RAISED BED GARDEN AND SUSTAINING ORGANIC VEGGIES AND PLANTS

THIS CHECKLIST INCLUDES:

- 10 items you will need to maintain your green fingered adventure.
- The highest quality Gardening items.
- Where you can buy these items for the lowest price.

The last thing we want is for your gardening project start to be delayed because you weren't prepared.

To receive your essential tool checklist, visit the link:

INTRODUCTION

'I grow plants for many reasons: to please my eye or please my soul, to challenge the elements or challenge my patience, for novelty or for nostalgia but mostly for the joy of seeing them grow.'

— DAVID HOBSON

A little over a decade ago, I bit into a tomato that I had just purchased from my local supermarket. It was perfectly formed, without bruise or blemish - it was also without taste. It looked totally different to those gnarled tomatoes that my grandmother used to grow in such abundance in her back garden, and which provided such mouth watering memories.

That perfect looking, store bought tomato awakened a memory that set me on a journey - a quest to reproduce some of the delights that my grandmother grew with such nonchalant ease. She was extremely proud of her vegetable garden and it was always filled with a seemingly endless variety of edible wonders.

I wanted to reproduce that garden and all the adventures that went into creating it. The trouble was, I had no idea where to begin. The large scale migration to cities and the transformation of our society that we have witnessed in the last few decades has seen a rapid demise in the gentle art of gardening. Today we pick up nearly all of what we eat on a quick trip to the local supermarket or greengrocer. Somewhere along the way, the very natural process of growing our own foods was transformed into a mystery – a dark art that many seem to believe is beyond the reach of all but trained specialists.

The objective of this book is to guide the reader on a journey similar to the one that I have been on for so many years now. Along the way I hope to show that gardening is neither difficult nor complicated. My grandmother had no horticultural training and was still growing much of her own food until she was well into her eighties. Using her notes and the additional information I have gathered over the years, I have put together this book to show just how easy gardening can be.

My desire is that this series of publications will do more than just teach you how to grow your own healthy and nutritious vegetables. I hope that, as in my case, you will become more concerned about what you eat and the processes that go into producing that food. As farming has become more industrialized, and as we have placed more and more responsibility for our food production into the hands of large corporations, the food that we put into our bodies, and the bodies of our children, has changed. Vegetables are now chosen for their shelf life and their visual appearance rather than for the nutrition they offer or the taste they provide. Much of what we eat will have travelled thousands of miles before it reaches our plates and all the way along that journey it is shedding its level of nutrition.

If nutrition levels and flavour were the only losses in these giant production processes, then it might be a price we are prepared to pay in exchange for the convenience offered. Unfortunately that is not the case. To a large extent, it is the environment that carries the burden of our desire for convenience. Don't think that the perfectly formed tomato that travelled several hundred miles to reach you is the result of careful plant husbandry and exposure to the best that Mother Nature has to offer. It will almost definitely have been grown in a greenhouse using an obscene amount of chemicals and unsustainable quantities of water. Those poor souls that picked and packed it for you will probably have been paid a subsistence wage, whilst working on tenuous contracts – all this so that you can have gorgeous looking produce at a low price, whilst making fortunes for large conglomerates.

I believe that growing your own food is so much more than just a matter of putting food on the table and saving yourself a few pennies. It is a passion, an art, an exercise and an act of rebellion against a system that does not have our best interests at heart.

You can join that rebellion. This series of books will guide you through the growing process from start to finish. As one book builds upon the information that you gained in another, you will, almost by accident, find yourself developing a broad-based horticultural knowledge. You will learn the tools you need as well as those that are just nice to have. You will follow the growing process from soil preparation, right through to harvest, with a little bit on storage and preservation thrown in for good measure. Above all, you will learn that gardening is not a lost art that disappeared along with our great grandparents. It is really very easy and requires little more than some basic techniques and a smidgen of enthusiasm. (If the enthusiasm is lacking don't worry – it will soon grow.)

I have learned many things in the course of my own journey. Much of what I discovered really surprised me. I didn't know, for example, how much pleasure could be gained from sprinkling a few seeds onto some damp compost in an old ice cream tub. The appearance of those first tiny leaves felt almost miraculous. Sitting down to a meal where every vegetable on the table was the result of my own labours was more rewarding than any three-star Michelin banquet.

There is something almost cathartic about plunging your hands into deliciously rich soil. Perhaps this is because, in doing so, we are returning to something that humankind has been doing for millennia. Something we were meant to do. We are retracing our roots back to their origins; back to a time before we got lost in the constant pursuit for more that seems to have gained such a grip on modern society. On this journey you will make many discoveries. You will learn that growing your own plants won't make you rich in ways that are now regarded as so important today. Instead you will discover an altogether new value system. Healthy food, exercise and the chance to engage in an activity that can be enjoyed by the whole family are things that are difficult to put a price on. I will leave it to you to judge their worth.

You will also learn that time has a different scale when gardening. Our lives seem to have become so rushed that merely slowing down has become almost impossible. Start gardening and you will learn that it is nature that dictates the pace and that hers is altogether different from your own. She won't be hurried, prodded or bribed.

This book is just one of a series of books that takes you across a whole spectrum of what is a very wide ranging subject. Most will start with an introduction to a specific subject so that you can get started as quickly as possible. There is nothing that kills desire more quickly than an overload of theory. After that there is a more advanced follow up that will take your knowledge to a higher level. I have deliberately avoided any subscribed order in which the series should be followed. Gardening should be fun and you are free to pick up those books on subjects that most please and motivate you. In writing these books, I did not set out to produce a dry theoretical masterpiece. Instead, I prefer to allow the reader to amble along the pathways of my own experience, making whatever detours and diversions he or she chooses to take along the way. As you are about to discover, this is a vast subject with many different ways of doing things. These books offer one route, but soon you will be experimenting and building ideas of your own, stealing methods from other gardeners and high jacking procedures from nature. That non-prescriptive way of learning is, in my opinion, what makes gardening such an interesting experience.

Finally, it would be unfair of me not to offer a word of caution from my own experience. Gardening is as addictive as nicotine or sugar, though without the health risks or weight gain. Dip just a toe into the water and the next thing you know you will be peering into neighbours' gardens, begging seeds and cuttings from total strangers and seeing allotments as educational opportunities. Previously nondescript window sills will metamorphose into greenhouses and you will begin to salivate at the sight of a tidy shed. Your dress sense will go all up the creek, or disappear altogether, and you will gather a collection of like-minded friends, the likes of whom you would never have met at that trendy wine bar on a Friday night. You have been warned.

1

WHY THE RAISED BED SYSTEM?

*H*umankind first started growing food deliberately in around 11 000BC. This is believed to have taken place on what is known as the Fertile Crescent that runs from the northern lip of the Red Sea to the Persian Gulf. Prior to that, our ancestors had been simple hunter gatherers, following herds or picking edible crops as and when they ripened. When the first crop cultivation started, it was an adaption that would change the face of history forever. Once we could control the process by which food was acquired and grow it, it enabled us to settle in one place. This would have profound ramifications on human society that are still being felt today.

As our ancestors began staying in one place for more extended periods, we could no longer rely on simple temporary shelters and fixed structures began to develop. By 9000 BC, we had begun learning to store grain and with this, food security increased. Though it took more effort to grow food than it did to harvest it from the wild, it meant that man could gather ten to one hundred times as many calories per acre as he had been able to in the past.

Suddenly people were producing more food in a day than they could actually eat in that time frame and they could keep it for leaner periods. Shortly after that, some people were able to step away from the food production process and develop other skills such as metal or woodwork. This then led to the barter system where some people were able to survive without being involved in the food production process at all. These might not seem like dramatic changes, but they would have a significant impact on the future.

On the Fertile Crescent, it was possible to grow food because the seasonal rains were so reliable. Soon, however, people further afield would begin using primitive but effective irrigation systems and food production became more widespread and moved to other areas.

All sounds good so far. No need to go racing after potentially nasty wild animals with a sharpened stick or be dependent on beating the birds to that wild fig tree you found last year. Just throw a few seeds onto the ground and pretty soon you could put your feet up and wait for your freshly baked bread rolls to be delivered.

Why then has one scientist described the introduction of agriculture as the 'worst thing in the history of the human race?'

The answer to that is that the arrival of managed cultivation opened the door for large scale agriculture, all be it, many thousands of years later. That has brought with it massive problems. Industrial food production incorporated the widespread use of harmful chemicals for both pest control and weed elimination. If you are going to squeeze every cent you can out of a production system, then all competition has to be seen as the enemy.

Whilst those developments were almost inevitable when producing food on the scale that we do today, we are starting to pay the price for our conversion from hunter gatherer to industrialized consumers. Mega food industries will tell you that the use of these chemicals and synthetic fertilizers is unavoidable if we are to continue to feed our burgeoning population. Many will dispute that argument, but trying to change the entire world economic system is probably a little outside the scope of this book. Instead, this first in a series of books sets out to offer an easy to master and inexpensive way to produce much of your own food yourself. In doing that you will at least be able to control the produce you put into your body and what goes into that produce. A large part of the process will fall back under your management, and you will be able to decide how free it should be of synthetic additives and pesticides.

The book does not propose to make you totally self sufficient, but it will guide you to a position where you can grow many of the vegetable crops that you and your family eat. If you do choose to extend what you learn in these pages to producing all of your own fresh produce - that is certainly not beyond the realms of possibility and hundreds of thousands of people around the world do exactly that.

Once you take over the growing of your own vegetables, you are assured that they are free from harmful chemicals and that they have not travelled many thousands of miles to reach your plate. Not only will you be reducing the size of your family's carbon footprint and eliminating exposure to toxic products, but you will also notice a very different taste from those store bought vegetables. Your own produce will be higher in vitamins and nutrients and have a far smaller adverse impact on the environment.

Raised bed gardening has become a very popular option for the home grower and there are many practical reasons for this which we will look at shortly. Over the years, people have moved away from gardening due to the changes that have taken place in society and the way in which we now lead our lives. As a consequence of this, people have lost a valuable skill and over time, what was once a normal day to day activity has begun to seem like something of a mystery. This book sets out primarily to show just how straightforward gardening can be, and the raised bed system will really add to that simplicity.

THE BENEFITS OF RAISED BED GARDENING:

- The first obvious benefit of raised bed gardening is the
  reduced physical effort placed on the gardener. Even if
  a bed is only nine or ten inches high, it means that the
  gardener doesn't need to bend so far and he or she can
  work the bed quite easily from a standing position or
  their knees if they choose to do so. Of course, the bed
  can be built higher and then even kneeling is not
  necessary. Gardening is, by nature, a physical
  occupation, but almost all of the aches and pain
  incurred are through bending rather than as a result of
  the digging or planting process. That is not to suggest
  that gardening has or will become a sedentary activity.

It merely means that it now requires effort that falls into the comfortable and sustainable exercise category rather than the extreme sports arena.

I like to build my beds to two feet as that is a comfortable height for me to work at, while at the same time giving me plenty of depth in which to lay in the growing medium for my plants.

For the disabled, raised beds can really be a game changer. From being an inaccessible past time, raised beds suddenly bring gardening back into the realms of possibility for those in wheelchairs or with bending difficulties. For people deprived of so many of the activities that most of us take for granted, this can really open a whole new window of opportunity.

- As a first time gardener, raised beds offer an easier system to manage. Much of the preliminary digging that takes place at the start of each season is eliminated. At the same time, many of the weeds that would typically be encountered are destroyed because you are not planting directly into the ground. They are not designed to make their way through such a depth of soil. That doesn't mean that you will never be troubled by weeds. That is one curse that the gardener will always have to bear. However, those that do manage to self seed are easily picked out as they won't have deeply established root systems. What's more, you can reach them easily and will not have to resort to crawling around on your hands and knees looking like and obsessive yoga guru.

- When you plant directly into the ground you must first either till the soil or you must deep mulch it and wait many months for that mulch to break down before you can plant. With this system, once the beds are prepared they are ready to plant and there is no tilling involved. Every year the gardener simply adds more compost and soil ameliorants, digs it over lightly and the bed is ready for replanting.

In recent years there has been much study into tilling soil and there is a growing movement that advocates not doing so at all. When we till soil we break down its natural structure which makes it prone to both wind and water erosion. Each year we lose 24 billion tonnes of fertile soil to erosion. That works out to a staggering 3.4 tonnes of our most important non renewable resource per person. While doing this, we release tonnes of carbon dioxide into the atmosphere and kill many of the beneficial micro organisms that the soil contains. Just one teaspoon full of healthy soil contains more micro organisms than there are people on the planet.

- This system offers another advantage over growing plants directly into open ground. Crop rotation is critical when planting into the ground. Each crop will reduce that soil of the nutrients that it most requires.

Over time a patch of soil can become so denuded that it can no longer support plants of certain kinds. On a large scale, vast quantities of fertilizer are used to replace this nutrient loss. Run off from excess chemical fertilizers is now a problem in many of the world's waterways and oceans. It also speeds weed growth thus leading to the use of excess herbicides. The commercial farmer can grow the same crop year after year in the same patch of ground because he is prepared to use synthetic fertilizer for all his plant nutrition.

To avoid this, crop rotation must be practised. In raised beds the soil is continually being topped up and having those nutrients replaced by good natural soil conditioners. Crop rotation simply ceases to be an issue. If you want to, you can plant the same crop in the same place for many years because, in effect, each time you plant you will be planting into new soil. This constant revitalizing of the growing medium is a crucial benefit in terms of raised beds and should not be underestimated.

As you delve deeper into this series, you will see that soil and its well being are crucial parts of the gardening process. Good soil is a valuable asset and, in short, if you don't have healthy soil, you won't grow healthy plants. That is, of course, unless you are simply prepared to replace the natural health of your soil with a vast cocktail of chemical ingredients. Unfortunately, most of the agro industry has now simply resigned to the fact that it will always use fertilizers to produce crops. The link between large scale farming and the chemical industries is now so entwined that it is difficult to see a way to separate them.

- Another advantage of raised beds is that pest control becomes a great deal easier. Flying pests will still need to be dealt with but other pests are far easier to manage. If you have ever gardened in an area where there are moles present then you will know what a nightmare they can be. They seem to have this incredible knack of snacking on the base of your root vegetables precisely one day before you had planned to harvest. When you arrive in the morning with your hopes high and a basket just begging to be filled, you suddenly discover that the carrots you had been nurturing for weeks are simply a pile of sad and withered leaves. If you do have moles then all you will need to do is lay a sheet of fine chicken mesh at the bottom of the bed before filling it and they won't get so much as a nibble from your crop.

Rabbits or deer may be a problem but the raised beds offer you something onto which you can easily attach netting to keep them out. The pests that most frustrate gardeners are slugs and snails. These ninjas of the night use an array of stealth tactics and an ability to stay up long after the weary gardener has gone to bed, to attack leafy crops. With a raised bed, sliding up the sides is already a deterrent, but you can increase the degree of difficulty by attaching a band of coarse shade cloth to make your bed into a natural fortress.

Flying insects are always going to find this system less of a deterrent than land bound critters. They will need to be subjected to all of the environmentally friendly pest control methods that you would use elsewhere in the garden and which we will look at in greater detail later in this series. The gardener's first defence against all pests, however, is his power of observation. An experienced gardener will know what signs to look out for, what plants are most vulnerable to attack and where about on the plant to find those signs. Raised beds are no substitute for experience, but they do at least bring the crops closer to the eye line. As with the deer and rabbit protection, raised beds are very easy to cover with hooped tunnels or shade netting and both of these options will help to protect against flying pests.

- The raised sides of a bed are exposed to the sun as opposed to planting into the grounds where the soil is cool. This can dramatically increase the growing season for your crops and that in turn will increase yields. Not only does the soil in your beds heat up earlier, but it also stays warm later. This allows you to get plants into the ground before you would if you were using conventional techniques, and then to keep growing longer.
- If you are blessed with perfect gardening soil then

drainage may not be an issue. (I have never met a gardener with perfect soil). Most people, however, need to really take drainage into consideration with traditional measures. It is something that is so often overlooked but which can lead to huge disappointment. Clay or a shallow sub soil layer can cause water logging and this really complicates the gardening process. Firstly it has to be dealt with which can delay the planting season. Secondly it takes longer to warm up and thirdly the clays tend to make the soil really difficult to work and far more physically demanding. If you have ever spoken to a gardener who has to work a heavy clay soil, you are likely to have heard him lament the problems that he has to overcome. He is always having to add sand and grit and each year he knows that the start of the season is going to be a difficult physical slog. What's more, if the weather suddenly goes dry, the clay can harden to a rock like consistency that plants struggle to deal with - with the exception of weeds of course.

In raised beds this is simply not an issue. You control the drainage by filling the bed correctly which you will soon see is very simple. After that drainage just isn't a problem and you can get straight down to planting your crops. You are no longer at the mercy of whatever type of soil it was that you happened to inherit. You are now master of the beds and in this godlike role you manage and you make up the soil so that it is in optimum condition at all times. This works for the gardener and it certainly works for the plants.

Even if you have the opposite problem and you are gardening on loose sandy soil where overly fast drainage is an issue, you can overcome it with this method. Though you control the planting medium in the actual beds, the soil beneath that may be fast draining. That problem can be overcome by applying a porous plastic membrane before you fill the bed. That will not stop drainage but it will slow it and in that way the problem is overcome. At the same time, the humus, compost and soil mix that you put into the bed holds moisture so you are assured of damp conditions that do not become overly waterlogged.

- Raised beds allow you to be far more targeted when it comes to watering. Traditionally it is just accepted that some water will be lost along paths which can also lead to erosion. As access is often tricky in normal beds, water is often sprayed quite long distances to reach the plants and this means that it does not always go where the gardener wants it to. Raised beds enable the gardener to water exactly where he wants the water to go and well managed soils hold moisture far better than lots of ground planted beds do. Water is becoming a precious resource and one that needs more consideration by all but especially the gardener who wants to work in collaboration with nature rather than against it.

- One of my favourite advantages of the raised bed system is that it enables the gardener to plant his crops far more densely than he otherwise might have. Because conditions are ideal, the gardener can plant many of his chosen vegetables more closely than he would if he were growing them in traditional rows in the ground. For one thing, he no longer needs to lose ground to footpaths running through the beds. With the raised bed method, and providing the beds have been built to the right size, the gardener has access from all sides of his bed and there are none of those narrow little paths creeping between the plants.

One of the options we will look at further into the book is to use what is called the square foot gardening method. This is a technique that was invented by an engineer called Mel Bartholomew many years ago and it simplifies the gardening process by breaking the bed into smaller more manageable chunks. You deal with one square at a time and research done over the years allows you to know precisely how many of each crop you can cram into each tiny square. This method dramatically eliminates inefficiency. For the inexperienced gardener it makes the whole process much less daunting as they are faced with just a small patch rather than a vast expanse. It becomes a simple case of breaking a large problem down into smaller and more manageable chunks. At the same time it leads to higher yields.

I hope that this overview of the raised bed system has at least allayed any fears you might have about growing your own produce. The whole purpose of the raised bed system is to make the gardeners life easier and it certainly does that effectively. Simply by choosing this method, you increase yields and reduce potential problems in one foul swoop.

If some of the back ache is taken out of the process then gardening becomes so much more of a pleasure and that is the way that it should be. For many people living in cities, contact with nature consists of an occasional walk in the park, at most. This method really can change that because there are few areas where you come into deeper contact with nature than you do with gardening. Suddenly you find yourself relating to nature at a whole different level than you do as a pure observer sitting on a park bench. You are now intimately involved in the whole process from preparing the environment for the plant through to germination, growth and harvest.

Your appreciation of soil is about to change dramatically. You will cease to see it just as brown dirt and will start to recognize it as the living, giving raw material that it really is. As you reconnect with nature in a way that you never have in the past, you will start to have a whole different appreciation of the food that you eat and what goes into producing it.

The beauty of this system is that you don't need acres of land. In South Africa there is a charity that works in impoverished townships. They teach a similar method and show people how they can grow enough food to supply the vegetable needs for a family of four from a bed the size of a front door.

As an education source for small children there can be few activities that a family can engage in together that will produce more significant rewards. That connection with nature is something that small kids love and everything from handling their first earth worm to seeing their first seeds sprout will be a new adventure for them. Add to that the delight of being able to eat something that they have played a part in producing, and you soon overcome that all too common distaste for vegetables. Serve a kid a store bought carrot that he had no part in producing and you will often face rejection of the vegetable. If they have helped plant the seed and do the watering and harvesting themselves, then parents are far less likely to encounter this problem. Theirs is the generation that is going to bear most of the brunt of what the agro chemical industry is doing to this planet and this type of education will be their greatest defence.

I recognize that I have tackled this subject purely from the vegetable production aspect. That is what raised beds are most commonly used for, but there is no reason that this system should not be used for growing ornamental plants just as effectively. I have always felt that the vegetable patch is an overlooked area when it comes to visual impact but it is entirely possible to use ornamental garden design principals when setting up your garden. Later in this series we will look at some of the design principles you can use that can make your vegetable patch as attractive as any ornamental garden. By combining beautiful flowering plants into your planting scheme, you can add aesthetic appeal and attract useful pollinating insects at the same time.

I am a firm believer that the age of the scruffy veg patch, tucked somewhere out of sight, is over. We should all be considering combining beauty and functionality and cease to see edible plants as being unsightly. A well laid out and flourishing vegetable garden is a sight to behold and that beauty is augmented when combined with other non-edible plants.

REASONS TO USE RAISED BEDS - RECAP:

- Less physical effort required
- Far easier to manage
- Greater control of growing medium
- No need for crop rotation
- Better pest control
- Greater heat retention
- Eliminates drainage issues
- Improved water management
- Denser planting affords greater yields

2

BEFORE STARTING

Raised beds are not a new invention. The pre-Hispanic people were using them as far back as 300 BC. Called Waru Waru, these beds were used because they solved the problem of soil erosion on the steep hills that these early gardeners were cultivating.

Though this concept of gardening hasn't really changed, the tools and equipment that we have at our disposal to make life easier certainly have. In this chapter we are going to look at some of the equipment you will definitely need, as well as some items that will just help make your gardening life that little bit less problematic. We will start with gardening tools and then we will move onto what you will need to make the raised beds themselves.

BASIC TOOLS:

Garden shears: Often called secateurs, this is one tool that you will use again and again and a good pair will last you a lifetime. In recent years I have watched the market get flooded with cheap shears and I can assure you that the money saved is just not worth it. There are basically two types of secateurs: the anvil type where the sharp blade meets a solid piece of metal in an almost crushing motion, and the bypass type. Bypass secateurs have two sharpened blades whose opposing faces slide past one another in the same way as a pair of scissors. These are far more effective at cutting green material whilst doing minimum damage to the plant.

It is essential when cutting branches and stems that the cut remains as clean as possible. This reduces the possibility that the wound becomes infected or contaminated. Better brands can be disassembled for easier cleaning and sharpening. As you will hardly ever venture into the garden without this piece of equipment I highly recommend a holster so that it can be hung from a belt.

Gloves: Even if you are not someone who likes to wear gloves when you are working, there are times when you will need to protect your hands. I like to have two pairs of gloves. One lighter pair protects from blisters and the like when doing lighter work. The other pair are heavy welders gauntlets and they come in handy when removing brambles or pruning roses or raspberries.

Shears: Although indispensable for the ornamental garden for such jobs as shaping topiary of trimming hedges, this is one tool that does not see much use in the context of raised bed vegetable gardening so if the budget is tight, leave it at the bottom of the list.

Garden fork: You will need this for loosening soil, turning over beds and lifting compost or manure. Look for a model that is sturdy and allows you to drive it in with your foot.

Hand trowels: These are tools that you will use on an ongoing basis to dig planting holes, carved seed rows or dig out weeds. They come in all sorts of shapes and sizes. You will use it often so look for a robust one that will last a long time. A medium size will do just about anything you ask of it.

Shovel: You are going to use this guy often as well so again look for quality. For jobs like moving compost from barrow to beds, the long handled French variety work best. The shovel comes in both flat nosed and sharp nosed versions. The main thing you want it that it is capable of lifting reasonably large quantities of material such as compost or soil.

Spade: Often confused with a shovel, a spade has a flat head and is used for digging rather than scooping. Here you don't want the long handle but rather the shorter English version with a handgrip on the end which you can push with the top of your thigh for that bit of extra leverage. Because it is going to be doing some heavy duty work make sure the handle is sturdy and that its design allows for you to drive it in with your foot.

Hoes: Essentially there are two types of hoe. The traditional one has a flat blade that you drive into the ground in a short cutting motion. The other is called either a draw hoe or a stirrup hoe which you pull toward you through the top half inch or so of soil. This is great for cutting off weeds at ground level. Both have their advantages but for annual weeds that you are most likely to encounter in a raised bed, the draw hoe version will be more effective. When making your purchase make sure that you will be able to buy replacement blades.

Rake: Once again there are two different types of rake. The spring tined, or lawn rake is exactly what the name suggests and won't help much in these types of beds. The ordinary garden rake comes with different sized heads. Choose a smaller size so that you can get in between plants to rake out dead material and spread mulch or top dressing.

Weeder: These are small tools designed to get in between plants and scrape out weeds. They come in all shapes and sizes and you should just choose one that suits you. Those that look like little flat bladed hoes work fine.

Trug: Trugs used to be open topped baskets made from woven wicker. Today they are more commonly made of plastic with two handles at the top. They are inexpensive and incredibly useful. I suggest buying two identical ones that fit inside one another. All the tools can be tossed into one and then the other can be used to gather weeds or crops once you harvest.

Wheelbarrow: If there is one essential item that gardeners get wrong more than any other, then in my opinion it has to be the wheelbarrow. These incredibly versatile pieces of equipment have been with us for hundreds of years since the Chinese first invented them for carrying their wounded off the battlefield. Today they come in every shape and size imaginable with folding options and two wheeled options thrown in for good measure.

Forget about what the salesman tries to sell you, this is what you need; a robust builder's barrow with one wheel at the front. Running around the front of that wheel there should be a metal bar or pipe. Don't buy it if it does not have this essential accessory. When you tip the barrow, you stand it on this metal piece and what you are carrying slides neatly where you want it to go. When you don't have it, the barrow remains balanced on its wheel which slides back toward you and hits you in the shin. It the proceeds to spread whatever you were transporting in any number of different directions.

Don't be tempted by a barrow with a solid rubber wheel and never touch one with an old metal wheel. It will sink into the soil and is ten times harder to push. Go for a heavy duty tyre with a tube. A one wheeled barrow is incredibly easy to manoeuvre and will allow you to carry a considerable amount of weight.

There is a vast array of ancillary equipment that can be useful and which you tend to acquire along the way. Old kitchen knives are great for dividing plants and getting weeds out of paving cracks. Balls of string are always needed somewhere, and no good gardener should be without a pocket knife.

Two words of warning when it comes to tools; the first is that, as with some many other things these days, suppliers will try to sell you some sort of a gizmo or tool for just about every conceivable situation. If you believe all that the publicity suggests, you will start finding yourself wondering how you ever survived without a battery powered dibber or a corkscrew weeding tool. The truth of the matter is that we have been gardening perfectly happily without most of these gadgets for millennia so start with the items listed above and don't purchase anything else until you have identified a genuine need. When you know that you are going to use a tool then buy the best one that you can afford. Car boot sales and garage sales are a great place to acquire tools cheaply.

The second thing is that garden tools are the sneakiest things you will ever come across. Give them half a chance and they will hide in the grass or find themselves an excellent shady position to lie around in and avoid doing any work. If ever you see a gardener wandering around in aimless circles, chances are he is searching for a trowel or weeder that he had in his hand just second earlier. I have known tools to slink off and not be seen again for years until suddenly found loitering amongst the compost or in the fork of a tree. One can of brightly coloured spray paint, used liberally on wooden handles, can save you hours of pointless searching and worrying whether or not you are suffering from early-onset dementia.

CONSTRUCTION BASICS:

Before starting actually to build your beds it would be a good idea to get everything you need in place for the job. First of all it is a good idea to decide what size beds you want and what material you want them to be made of. Here you are spoiled for choice and three distinct mindsets start to become evident. The first is the person who just wants to get started and who is willing to pay reasonably exorbitant amounts for purpose built raised beds made from hardwood and delivered as a flat pack.

The second distinct class of gardener is the perpetual recycler who believes that purchasing anything but the most essential items is somehow cheating. All of his beds tend to be made from old pallets, side panels of wrecked cars and mismatched second hand doors retrieved from a skip.

Somewhere between these two extremes is the average gardener who is prepared to buy most of what is needed but is working to a budget.

Firstly it might be a good idea to point out that none of these approaches is wrong and that the plants don't actually care. They tend to be quite un-elitist and are, for the most part, far more likely to get picky about soil conditions and climate than they are about what materials the beds are made of.

Now it is just up to you to decide which of these three categories you fall into. Raised beds can be made from any material that will support the weight of the soil and which will resist rotting in an exposed outdoor environment. Materials that work well include brick, cinder block, corrugated iron sheeting, railway sleepers and wood. Your choice will often be governed as much by what is readily available as anything else.

By far the most common material used is wood. Wood is attractive, reasonably easy to work with and most widely available. Assuming that this is the material that you want to work with, then it now only remains to work out the quantities that you will require. You need to start with the size of the beds you want and the depth. You also need to consider how to avoid as much waste as possible. I often use planks that are eight foot long, nine inches wide and two inches thick. This also just happens to be a very standard material for scaffolding boards so is a size that can be bought off the shelf at most merchants.

The reason I choose that size is that beds that are four feet wide are easy to work because they only require me to reach two feet into the bed from each side. By cutting my planks in half to obtain the end pieces I eliminate waste altogether. That means that for a bed of one plank depth, I require three boards - one for the ends and one for each side. I prefer to go a little deeper so six planks gives me eighteen inches of depth which is almost perfect.

Of course, the choice of wood is another matter. Standard scaffold boards tend to be made from pine which is one of the cheapest options but is not the longest lasting. Cedar lasts much longer, and though more expensive, is worth the extra investment. Rough sawn timber is cheaper than prepared wood and is perfectly acceptable for this operation. Rough sawn timber is the wood directly from the sawmill before being planed. The best way to source your timber is to order it directly from a timber yard rather than from a retail outlet. Because most yards are familiar with cutting to scaffold board size they don't need to alter their saw to accommodate your order. Just be sure that you know all of your dimensions and quantities in advance.

The price of wood varies depending on what is available in the area. In some places rough sawn hardwood such as oak can prove cheaper than softwood, so explain to the saw mill what you want to do and ask them what they suggest.

Once you have decided the size and shape of your beds you can do the calculations. Eight feet is by no means the longest length to which you can build a bed, but bear this in mind; the soil is going to put pressure on the wood and the longer you build the beds the more they are likely to bow out. It is quite easy to attach braces but you may be better off making two eight foot beds rather than one sixteen foot one. Also don't feel that you design should be limited to square or rectangular blocks. T and L shapes are not difficult to make and add further design possibilities. Just be sure to stick to sizes that make reaching across the bed easy otherwise you lose one of the major benefits of this system. Two foot is a comfortable distance to reach for the average person.

To add stability, it is common to add corner braces and one or two braces down the inside or the outside of the sides. This can be done with lengths of two by three which is another very standard timber size.

People will suggest that you use pressure treated timber, often referred to as tanalized. There is no doubt that this will add years to the life of your beds but the treatment includes a cock-tail of nasty chemicals. Whilst there is no evidence that these can be transferred to the crops you are growing, it is wise prac-tise to avoid the risk.

If you can get hold of reclaimed railway sleepers they make the most sturdy and long lasting beds. They too have been treated with bitumen but many have been exposed to weather for years. If I get them I line the inside of the bed with plastic membrane before filling so that I am sure I will get no leaching. When considering your options, understand that large timber such as sleepers requires heavy lifting and needs to be cut with a chain saw.

For most timber, a battery powered circular saw is perfect for doing your cuts and if that isn't in your tool kit then a hand cross cut saw will do the work and save you several trips to the gym. You will need suitable screws of a length two and a half times the thickness of your planks. Treated deck screws or stainless steel screws will add considerably to their longevity. If your budget extends to it you can use galvanized coach bolts instead of screws as theses are much more substantial.

Use a battery drill that doubles as a screwdriver then you just need one tool to do both jobs. Pre-drill your holes with a bit appropriate to the screws you have. You can purchase a counter sunk bit for very little and this ensures that the countersink and pre-drilling are all done in one operation.

Other tools you will definitely need are a long tape measure and a spirit level. The tape can also be used for checking for square but if you have a large builder's square this will speed that process. Don't buy one just for this job.

You now have enough equipment to build your beds. Some people like to line the inside of their beds with plastic membrane so that the wood is not always exposed to the damp soil. The problem with this system is that the water tends to sneak in between the planks and the membrane, and you then have a situation where the wood is both damp and cannot breathe. I prefer to use a non toxic penetrating wood treatment and paint all four sides of each plank with two coats.

Another individual choice is to drive corner stakes into the ground for additional strength. If the braces are in place securely this is another step that I do away with. Once the bed is squared up and filled with a couple of tons of soil it is not going to move.

You now have the basic materials for building the beds on site and you are ready for the next step. We will look at filling the completed beds in the next chapter but you are going to need good quality top soil. If you buy a bagged product and you have several beds this can soon become expensive. You are better off using loose top soil delivered as a truck load as this makes for a considerable saving. Because you cannot always rely on a speedy delivery in this situation, it is probably a good idea to order that now. Work out the volume that your beds will contain and order half of that from your local nursery or anyone else that offers good top soil. Swimming pool builders and people digging foundations often will sell a truckload at very reasonable prices. Soil is a valuable resource and if you have the place to store it then it is a wise idea to order slightly more than you think you will need. It always comes in handy somewhere.

If you are only building a very small raised bed, then garden centres sell bags of soil but in this case you won't need to buy it until we get to the next phase of the operation.

Irrigation is another option to consider as it makes your life considerably easier and reduces the amount of water that you will use. Many of the systems can be incorporated after the beds have been built but if the system you choose needs to be installed before the soil mixture going in then that too will need to be on-site before you start work. One other luxury is a greenhouse. It is undoubtedly not something that you need right away, but if you can gain access to one it will broaden your ability to grow crops and other plants over a more extended period. Book nine in this series will give you a more comprehensive look at greenhouses in general.

TOOL AND CONSTRUCTION – RECAP:

- For the garden you will mainly need hand tools
- A basic collection of hand tools will get you started. You can expand this if you need to but start small
- For construction you will need tools appropriate to the material you choose for the beds
- Beds can be made from any number of different materials according to both taste and budget
- You will need to weigh up whether or not to do the construction yourself

3

LOCATION AND SET-UP OF A RAISED BED GARDEN

*I*n this chapter we are going to look at where to place your raised bed and what factors to take into account when making that decision. After that we will take a look at putting the raised bed together and the best products to use for building it and filling it.

When positioning your raised beds there is room for flexibility. It stands that you would want to try to achieve optimal placing; but that is just not always practical or possible. For instance, you can place raised beds on patios, balconies and even in greenhouses. You may not be able to achieve all of the growing criteria under these conditions, but that certainly does not mean that you should miss out on the pleasure, and benefits that gardening offers you.

Ideally, a raised bed should be placed on level ground and receive a minimum of eight hours per day of sunlight. By aligning your beds on a north south axis, you ensure that the beds receive the maximum amount of light possible. As the sun passes over from east to west the least amount of shade is given by those plants that you have in the bed. That will provide near perfect light conditions for growing most vegetables. The next crucial consideration is access to water. People often underestimate just how important this factor can be and imagine that they can just do the watering with watering cans. Carrying a heavy watering can once or twice may not seem too daunting a task, but when you have to do it twice a day for six months or more, it suddenly becomes a herculean effort. Putting an obstacle like this in your way will eventually kill your enthusiasm and place the whole project at risk. Your bed needs to be at least close enough to a tap that you can run a hosepipe to it. If you are able to trap water off the roof of your house in a water butt or tank then consider buying a small electric pump so that you can simply pump that free water to where ever it is needed.

Access is another important consideration. You will need to be able to approach the bed pushing a heavily laden wheelbarrow, so build that into your planning when choosing the final position. Ideally you would like to avoid stairs, steep slopes or overly narrow paths. That may not be possible if you live on a slope, but there is nothing to stop you setting out your beds in a kind of terrace system with a path that winds down along the contour lines.

Of course, there are going to be situations where it is simply not possible to meet all the ideal criteria If, for example, you are putting a raised bed onto a balcony, the building will probably cause shade at some time during the day. What that may mean is that you will need to be more selective about the plants that you choose to grow. Some vegetables and herbs require less light, and then there are ornamental plants that are perfectly happy growing in shade. It is all just a question of adapting to those conditions that you cannot change.

Once you have chosen the position that offers you the best conditions for your raised beds, it is time to do some planning. This is the step that so many people either skim over or miss out altogether. People are keen to get on with the job and start moving forward as soon as possible. I believe it is for this reason that we see so many vegetable gardens that are purely functional but lack aesthetic appeal, and it really isn't necessary. A vegetable garden can be a thing of great beauty and raised beds enhance that because the plants are much closer to eye level than in lower beds. You may choose to go down the purely functional route, and that is fine, but don't go there just because you were in too much of a hurry to spend a few hours planning.

First of all, measure out the area that will become your vegetable garden. There is no need for extreme accuracy so you can probably just pace it out. Once you have done that, do a scale drawing on an A4 piece of paper and then just do some sketches and experiments to see what your options are. There are some templates at the end of this book and for more visual inspiration, take a browse through some garden magazines and surf the internet a little. An excellent way to get inspiration is to visit some of the better known public gardens where you will see design used in inspirational ways. When you have seen just what can be achieved with well designed raised bed gardens, you will be glad that you took the extra time.

Another factor to take into account is that garden design is beginning to change because of changing global weather. There is a move away from the large rolling lawns of the past. This space is now being turned over to water wise planting and productive beds like the ones you are considering, where both soil and water can be better managed. Over the next few decades, though it is likely that lawns will not disappear alto-gether, their dominance of the landscape will be far more restricted. It is often the lawn that demands most in terms of maintenance time, chemicals and water. All of this to produce what is, in nature's terms, just a vast area of monoculture that is not conducive to any form of biodiversity. Design is an important aspect to all garden preparation and in book seven in this series we will be going into the design process at greater length.

In your design consider different shapes of bed as well as combining them with other garden features such as flower beds, ponds and nice seating areas. Why should your raised bed garden be purely functional when, with no extra cost, you can turn it into a visual oasis that just happens to produce wonderful healthy food? One advantage of a well thought out design is that you can grow into it. You may not immediately be able to put in all of those raised beds, or that pond of your dreams, but if it is on your drawing and you have planned for it, it can be added later. Because you already know where it will go, the design will be cohesive and not just a higgildy piggildy mess where each addition looks like the after thought that it was.

Remember when drawing up your design to consider access. Beds should not be more than four feet wide. If you build up against a fence or wall, narrow the bed width to two feet as you won't be able to access both sides of the bed. That doesn't mean that you are restricted to squares and rectangles. Throw in some T shapes or right angle turns. Even a U shaped bed can be both practical and attractive. Changing the height of the beds can also add another pleasing design dimension. This is a chance to be daring and stamp your signature on a garden that may well be with you for many years. You are no longer obliged to follow the dull rectangular layout that our ancestors used. Instead you can go a little wild whilst still remaining within the boundaries of practicality.

Paths need to be carefully considered too, when drawing up your plan. Never make paths narrower than the width of a wheel barrow and if you can make them a little wider to aid manoeuvrability then do so. You are going to be using those paths regularly, so you don't want them turning into muddy quagmires. That entails typically surfacing them with something. This need not be expensive. The timber yard where you bought your wood may well be quite happy to get rid of those wood chips that they create in such abundance. Other options include gravel, broken roof tiles and building rubble. I have even worked in a garden where there were so many stones that I could just grab a few bucketfuls of them as I worked and cast them along the pathways as I went along. Eventually they gave me a wonderful gravel path and for free while at the same time loosening up the soil in the beds. Again, the choice of materials is related to your budget and if you have a substantial one you could consider paving or concreting those areas that you will be walking along so frequently. Concrete is labour intensive but leaves you with a long lasting and solid path. Again, with a little thought and ingenuity, even a plain concrete path can be transformed into something attractive. Both brushed concrete and pebble mosaic techniques are easy to master and make cheap aesthetic additions.

Once you are happy with your design, it is time to start putting it all together. The first thing you will need to do is to take a good look at the ground on which you will be placing the bed. If it is grassy then you will have to lift the turf before you start. Unfortunately this can be a bit of a back breaking job. The best way to tackle this task is with a sharp spade, cutting underneath the turf and lifting spade sized pieces off to expose the bare earth underneath. Set these sods aside as they will come in useful at a later stage. If the chosen plot is covered in weeds then these can simply be pulled out by hand. Don't waste them either. They will make a great start for the compost heap that you will eventually create. You will discover as you venture deeper into this subject, that gardeners are highly adept at reusing all sorts of materials that most people wouldn't have considered. If you are time rich and don't intend to start building the garden immediately, you can cover the ground with black plastic sheeting and the grass and weeds will weaken considerably due to light deprivation. When you need to clear them, the task will be that much simpler.

Once you have cleared the ground where the raised bed is to be placed, dig it over to a depth of about six inches using a garden fork. This is simply to maximize drainage. After that rake it over lightly, and then you can lay your spirit level on it in a couple of places and see that it is level. If it is not, it may be that you are easily able to achieve a level simply by raking some soil from the higher patches to the lower ones. If the incline is more serious then you will need to dig down the higher ground until a level can be achieved. The reason that level ground is essential is that soil in a sloped bed will put greater pressure on the lower walls of the bed and that will reduce their lifespan.

At this point, it is probably a good time to look at the different options that are available to you from which to build your project. Much will depend on what materials are readily available, your skill levels and the time you have. Permanent structures made from brick or cinder block both work well. You will need to cast a concrete foundation and wait for it to set but it doesn't have to be very deep as you are unlikely to be building to a height of more than two feet. Working with bricks and blocks requires different tools to woodwork and you will need to get the hang of basic brick laying, as well as purchasing sand, stone and cement.

If you are near a quarry or have access to quantities of stone, this too can give you an attractive bed that will last a long time. Stone walls can be held together using cement or they can be dry stone walls.

Wood is probably the most commonly used material in raised bed building. Eventually it does rot, but if you use a good timber like cedar and you treat it with a non-toxic preservative you are likely to get many years of service from each bed.

Other materials include woven willow or wattle. This is an easy to use material if you have access to it. Stakes are driven into the ground every 12 inches and then lengths of the weaving material are simply threaded between them in a basket weave manner. This is a very attractive option that was widely used in the medicinal gardens of European monasteries during the Middle Ages. Such beds can be built up to a height of two feet, which is generally as deep as you would need your beds to be. The product does not have a very long life span and you should not bank on getting more than three or four seasons from it. The inside can be lined with a plastic membrane or landscape fabric which will reduce drainage through the sides and help increase the life span of the bed.

Railway sleepers are long lasting, attractive and provide a really solid bed that will last for years. Used railway sleepers are becoming harder to source these days, but there are now timber companies that have recognized this gap in the market. They have turned to cutting sleeper sized timbers with gardeners in mind, and they often sell their produce through garden centres. Whilst they are not strictly true railway sleepers, they offer the same advantages without the bitumen products that were used in the original preservation process. Disadvantages are that there will be some heavy duty lifting involved in the construction process and unless you have a really big circular saw they will need to be cut with a chain saw. They will also be pricey, so you will need to decide if their longevity outweighs the cost. If you can overcome the down side, you will have a wonderful bed that will serve you well for many years.

Plastic planks are a relatively new possibility. Produced using recycled plastic, these boards can be screwed onto wooden or even metal, posts in the same way as wooden boards would be. This is a long lasting option but you will need to install support posts at regular intervals as they tend to bow under pressure. This is not a huge effort and if you can access this material at a reasonable price, then it is one that you may want to consider.

Another possibility using plastic is a fit together kit that you assemble yourself. These take the form of blocks that clip together, a little like a child's Lego kit. Being plastic they will last for many years but unless the designers have made some changes recently, they tend to bow out at the joints due to the soil pressure. The colour range is also quite limited and tends to be a little incongruous with the natural finish that most people would hope for in a garden. That may well improve as use of this product expands. They clip together really quickly and you can have your bed up in just a couple of hours.

There are also pre-made wooden kits that you assemble yourself and which are made from red cedar. These are delivered as a flat pack. Though not cheap, they are easy to assemble and they eliminate the use of tools such as the circular saw. Some manufacturers will produce these to your dimensions so that you can choose the design rather than being dictated to by limited shapes and sizes.

The final option is to hire a professional to build the beds for you. All landscapers will be familiar with this sort of work and have the requisite tools. Most of them are familiar with garden design so they could help you from that aspect as well. If you are choosing wood, and there is not a landscaper available, then it is easily within the scope of any carpentry company.

Obviously, there will be extra costs if you are hiring outside professionals. You will need to decide for yourself whether having the job done so that you can focus on the gardening aspect warrants that expense. Many people these days suffer from time poverty and this may be the quickest way forward for them.

Finally there is the recycled bits and pieces option. I have seen beds made with woven pieces of cast off hosepipe, sand bags, recovered fishing nets, old doors and driftwood. With a little artistic wizardry, any number of materials can be used. The point here is not so much what you make your beds with, but the fact that this system is so flexible. As long as what you are using can contain the weight of damp soil, and is non-toxic, it can be used for this purpose.

Despite the vast array of options, most beds will be made from planks. They are attractive to the eye, widely accessible and fairly easy to convert into raised beds. Most of the assembly work only requires a minimum of carpentry know how, and the average home handyman will cope easily. Whatever route you choose to go down, be aware that the soil does exert a lot of pressure and the beds need to be strong enough to support that. A simple brace, screwed firmly down from one side of the bed to the other will often be all that is needed to prevent the planks from bowing outwards. A more attractive option is to attach a top frame. This is a wooden frame that is fastened to the top of the bed but with the planks laid flat rather than on their sides. The frame needs only to be about four inches wide so you can just split some of the same size boards that you used for the sides up the middle using your circular saw. Because the top frame is flat it adds considerable strength while at the same time giving a nicely finished appearance to your creation.

Once your beds are made and in position, check them for square. Beds of this size easily distort. You can either use a builders setting out square or a tape measure for this job.

Measure diagonally from corner to corner and once you are getting the same size measurement across both diagonals, then your bed is square. If they are out of square don't be too concerned. As long as your dimensions were all cut to the correct size then you will be able to get them to square up with a little prodding and gentle persuasive kicking. If they aren't strong enough to sustain a bit of nudging at this stage, they won't cope with the wait that the growing medium will exert on them later.

PRE-PLANNING AND POSITIONING – RECAP:

- Consider the position and the slope of the ground
- Aim to position the beds to run from north to south where feasible
- Consider access to water and distance from the house or shed
- Focus on a design before doing any work. The garden does not have to be purely functional
- Consider the materials available and what works best for you. Wood, stone, brick, railway sleepers, woven willow and plastic are all options as are reclaimed materials
- Bear in mind the soil will put pressure on the sides
- Consider size of paths and materials they could be made from

4

FILLING THE BEDS

inally, your design is finished, your plot is cleared and your bed frames assembled. It is now time to start filling your beds so that you can get down to growing some crops. The success of your harvest depends on what you now do. You might scrimp and save on the frame of the beds but the growing medium is essential. Firstly decide if you need to lay a mesh into the bottom of your beds. You will do this if you suspect that mice, moles or other rodents are going to try to enter from ground level.

Next decide if you are going to need to place a membrane to slow the drainage of water. You will only need to do this if you are on really sandy soil and you will have been easily able to deduce this while you were preparing the ground. Some people like to use a weed proof membrane to stop unwanted plants taking advantage of the beautiful growing conditions and suddenly making an appearance in their carefully laid out planting scheme. If your beds are deep, this is unlikely to happen. Weeds that attempt to grow through two feet of soil are unlikely to make it to the surface, and even if they do, they will be in such a weakened state that they will be easy to deal with. In shallower beds, it is possible that some weeds will make their way to the surface and so some sort of a membrane will prevent this. You can purchase weed proof membrane from most garden centres. This allows water to penetrate but prevents plants from doing so. Many gardeners simply layer the bottom of their beds with old sheets of corrugated cardboard made by flattening boxes. These are free and will breakdown eventually, but by then any resident weeds will have almost definitely have died.

If you feel you need to line the sides of the beds with a water-proof membrane then now is the time to do so. You can purchase heavy duty plastic from most builders' merchants and this can simply be stapled to the insides of the bed with a good industrial stapler. Once the soil is added it will hold the liner in place effectively. Pond liners are another option but they are usually more expensive.

Once you have decided which of these options to go for and fitted the relevant materials, you are free to start putting in the bottom layer. This is the drainage layer and you have a wide choice of options available. You can purchase gravel but although it will do the job it will need to be delivered and it costs money. If you prefer the free option, then you can use old sticks, brush, grass clippings or even small logs. In short, that bottom layer can consist of any organic material that is free draining as your plants will be growing in the layer above. This is a great time to get rid of those sods that you dug up and put aside. They can be turned upside down and laid back into the bed grass and all. After that just stomp them flat and lay in whatever layer is going in next.

A brief warning when filling the bottom layer; use composed or semi composed plant matter. Lawn clippings are a good example. Once they have started to break down and formed almost a compost themselves, they are ideal for the bottom of raised beds. The breaking down process of green material uses nitrogen, so if you throw in large amounts of green matter such as lawn or hedge clippings, it will deplete the layer above of this important plant nutrient. After just a few weeks those clipping will have broken down enough to no longer to pose a threat in this way. This means the green clippings will need to have been composted or you will need to allow the material to break down in the beds before adding the soil.

It is the top twelve inches of your new beds where all the action is going to take place and this is where you want your soil to be in peak condition. There is any number of recipes out there for you to try but this one will stand you in good stead. Aim for forty percent homemade garden compost, forty percent soil and twenty percent sharp sand. Many people tend to overcomplicate this process and it really doesn't need to be too complicated at all. Soil is a living, breathing, organism that we all too often overlook. As you become more involved in the process of gardening you will begin to see it as your most precious resource. Throughout this series of books you will pick up tips on how to enhance the condition of your soil. If your soil is not healthy then your plants won't be healthy. Much of the agricultural industry has so degraded their soil that they can no longer grow crops without adding vast amounts of chemical fertilizer. As an organic gardener you won't want to go down that slippery path, and proper soil management is the only way to avoid it.

The compost is high in nutrients, especially if manure was used in the process of making it. I always include some form of manure when making compost because it provides me with that high nutrient level that my plants need. It will help to feed the plants and it acts like a sponge at the same time, so it will help retain moisture. The sand is simply to ensure that things don't get clogged up and that drainage remains free flowing. What you are aiming for is a dark crumbly mix that feels slightly damp and cool.

This is one of the cheapest ways to fill your beds. If you were unable to purchase top soil, or if it was prohibitively expensive, you might be able to scrape the top layer from what will now become your paths. It is only wasted where it is at the moment and so you can shovel it up and toss it into the beds and then replace it with an easy to walk on material like wood chips. Often your topsoil will include some garden weed seeds. They will generally sprout quickly and be easy to deal with by hand. If you are unfortunate enough to have lots of weeds then you may have to revert to covering the soil with black plastic for a fortnight once it is in the bed. This will weaken any seeds that survive.

The compost that you use should be well broken down and you may need to buy it if you don't already have some. As soon as you start gardening, one of the first things you will be doing is making your own compost so in future you should be able to top up beds from your own supply. If you have access to well rotted manure then you can augment the mix with that. Halve the amount of compost and replace it with the manure. A word of warning about manure; if it is still fresh it can burn your plants so set it aside for a few months until it has time to mature. Most farmers have plenty of manure and they can often be persuaded to drop you off a trailer load. If you have this option, then grab it even if you can't use the manure immediately. It is one of those resources that gardeners can never have too much of. Don't worry if it comes with loads of straw in it. It all just adds to the cocktail that your plants will delight in. Well rotted manure does not smell bad, contrary to public opinion.

Fill the beds until the contents are literally bulging out over the top and then let everything sit for around two weeks. Fairly quickly you will notice the whole heap beginning to subside as it settles into its new home. What you have done is created a perfect environment in which plants will thrive. Over time the materials in the bed will continue to subside though not at the same rate as they did over the first fortnight. Don't be alarmed at this. It is part of the natural decomposition process and you will be regularly adding to it to keep it in perfect condition.

There are many other recipes for filling the beds, and one which you will see often replaces the compost with peat. There are places in Canada where peat is being produced by nature faster than it can be harvested, but in much of the rest of the world, and certainly in the United Kingdom and Europe, peat extraction is not sustainable and is causing severe environmental problems, including releasing methane gas into the atmosphere. There are alternatives such as coconut Coir and rice husks which are bi-products of the agricultural industry. Still, as gardening starts to grow from a hobby into an obsession, you will find that more and more of what you need can be obtained from your own resources. You will be producing your own compost and gathering fallen leaves to make leaf mould. Soon buying things like Coir will mostly become a thing of the past.

If you can resist the urge to start growing things in your new beds immediately, then letting them sit for a fortnight or even longer, is a good idea. Another thing that you can do is to test your soil so that you know precisely how acid or alkaline it is. This can be done by sending a sample to a laboratory or by using a home testing kit. Ideally you want to have a PH of six to seven, which is ideal for growing most vegetables. In the regions of five to eight should not see plant growth being inhibited in any way. Although it may be comforting to test your soil, correcting it can be costly and often involves the use of chemical additives. As you are mixing the growing medium yourself, you are sure that all the ingredients are natural and it is highly unlikely that it will fall outside of the above PH levels. With experience, you will reach a point where you can judge whether a soil will provide an excellent growing medium just by picking up a handful and rolling it around in your hand.

FILLING THE BEDS – RECAP:

- Before starting to fill, decide if you want to line the sides or place a mesh against rodents such as moles
- The top thirty centimetres are the most important. The lower section can be filled with most vegetable materials as it will break down eventually
- Think about drainage
- Buy good soil and mix it with good ameliorants such as compost or well-rotted manure
- Try to let filled beds sit for a fortnight before planting
- Test your soil if you are not sure of its quality

5

WHAT TO PLANT WHEN

*T*his is the part of the process that you have probably been looking most forward to. After all that effort, you are now at a point where you can decide what plants you want to grow and what methods best suit your situation. Should you plant seeds directly into the soil or should they be started in trays? Should you be starting out with seeds or would you be better off with seedlings? More importantly, what plants should you choose?

The last question is probably the easiest to answer so we will begin there. The best vegetables to grow are those that you eat on a daily basis. An excellent place to start is with your weekly shopping list. Items that are most likely to appear are onions, tomatoes, lettuce and beans. After that you probably buy the odd cabbage, carrots and peas. All of these make good choices for your planting plan and that planting plan is crucial. Potatoes are another staple of our diets but I will get to that as some alternative methods can save you time and space.

Draw to scale an outline plan of your beds. You probably have this already from when you laid out your design. You will want to make several photocopies of this and perhaps consider some sort of file that you can keep them in. Onto this plan you will mark what crops are going in and when. You will also be able to give a rough estimate of when you hope to harvest so that you know what space will become available for either a second sowing of the same crop or a different crop. Each season you will fill out a new plan and make adjustments according to how successful certain crops were, how much excess you had and any problems that you encountered. If, like me, you are not the greatest record keeper, this may seem a little long winded and unnecessary. Over the years I have learned that records are crucial to improving my results and making me a better gardener. I keep both a daily diary and the garden plans that I worked on in previous years. With these I am able to look back and see what cultivars and varieties worked most effectively, what pests or diseases I encountered and even what the weather patterns were like. As you build up this catalogue of records you will start to become more effective at choosing your crops at the start of the season. I start my gardening day by going through the diary of that date during previous years and almost invariably it reminds me of some chore that I should be doing or something that I should be adding to my planting list. I now have records going back ten years and it is difficult to overstate their importance. Gardening requires such a wide variety of different tasks to be performed by the gardener that it is easy to overlook something that may later turn out to have been important. Record-keeping helps build up a catalogue of things to be done and plants that worked or didn't work.

The more comprehensive you make your records, the more valuable they will be. Each year you will visit plant markets and nurseries and have catalogues drop into your letterbox. At first, you will be like a child let loose in a sweet shop. There will be so many choices available to you that it will be difficult to make up your mind. The temptation to try out that exotic new tomato, that strange-looking pepper or that different coloured potato, will be almost overwhelming. I am not suggesting that you should ever lose that sense of wonder and excitement. Every year a portion of my planting plan is dedicated to exotic experiments. Some have been a delight and others a total wipe out. It is only through record-keeping that I am able to keep track of the stalwarts - the plants that I know are going to cope with local conditions and produce a reliable crop season after season. The produce I grow is an integral part of what goes onto my table and I can't afford the time, effort and expense of too many failed experiments. Unfortunately, the nursery industry has become as cutthroat as any other, and there is always competition to come up with the next new idea and the next so-called wonder plant. Very often they don't live up to the sales hype that accompanies them and, whilst it may be novel to have a black tomato on your plate, if it tastes watery or bland you may be disappointed.

Another thing that you will discover is that many of the seed companies are owned by the same handful of large corporations who dominate much of the industry. They patent their seeds and cross-breed in search of the new wonder variety of the year, but often you will not be able to harvest your own seed from the crop because they do not come true to form on a second sowing. These seeds are known as F1 hybrids. Many of these F1 varieties will produce a very good harvest the first year and it is by keeping good records that you will know whether to purchase new seed and sow the same crop the following year.

One real positive advance over recent years has been that of the heirloom seed movement. These are people who specialize in and are passionate about, reintroducing seeds that have gone out of fashion. It is here, that you are most likely to rediscover those old fashioned tomatoes that your grandmother used to grow or that runner bean that seems impossible to locate anymore. These crops may lack the perfect aesthetic appeal that many supermarket crops have, but they will more than make up for it in terms of taste and shelf life. What is more is that you will be able to harvest your own seed for free and repeat the results in years to come. Many gardening clubs support the heirloom seed movement and I cannot stress how valuable these clubs are, both as a source of information and as a place at which to swap seeds, seedlings and even some of your excess harvest.

The reason that antique seeds have become so rare is that seed companies stopped promoting them. There were two reasons for this. One was that the demand for perfect looking vegetables grew as people left the land and moved to cities. The companies simply responded to that demand. Once people lost their connection with the land, they came to assume that a misshapen vegetable was not as good to eat as perfectly looking one. This has resulted in huge amounts of food waste as perfectly edible vegetables are thrown away, simply because they failed to meet the aesthetic requirements of the supermarkets and their clients. This, in turn, has led to another movement called the ugly vegetable movement which is trying to persuade buyers to purchase these slightly deformed crops.

Food that is not perfect looking is no less nutritious than that is. In fact, the opposite is often true. Vegetables are bred for form and colour rather than taste, as the supermarkets realized that people made their purchases based primarily on what they saw. Gradually we have come to believe that gnarled carrots or misshapen tomatoes are not as tasty or are inferior in some way. When breeding plants for a specific requirement, such as how they look, we often lose other benefits in the breeding process and it is frequently taste that is forfeited first. When we start going back to non-hybrid seed, we generally regain some of the qualities that were once taken for granted.

The second reason non modified seed fell out of use was that seed companies discovered that if they made minor adjustments to a plant, either through cross-breeding or genetic modification, then they were able to take out a patent on that seed. Obviously, there were higher profits to be made on seed to which they owned sole rights, and gradually the unpatented seed just fell from our collective memories. It was simply not subjected to the massive marketing tactics applied to patented crops.

Because seeds are often the cheapest way to grow vegetables, and because they offer a natural place to begin, we will start by looking at growing some of your plants from seed. Some seeds remain viable for decades and others won't last for long. There are even examples of botanists being able to grow plants from seed found in Egyptian pyramids while parsnips grow best from seed that is fresh. When purchasing packets of seed, you almost always end up with more seed than you can use in a single sowing. Gardeners cannot throw away seed. It is simply genetically impossible for someone who grows plants to throw these valuable little life sources into the garbage. The result is that if you are not careful, you will end up with a vast collection of seed. As a rule of thumb don't plant seed that is older than three years and always label and date stored seed clearly. Keep it in a plastic box such as a used ice cream container and store it in a dark cupboard. One advantage of associating with other gardeners is that you can share or swap seeds and thus avoid the trauma of deciding what to do with all that excess that you inevitably acquire. This also means that you naturally start to build variety into your planting.

Some seed comes coated in clay to allow for easier handling and others come embedded into a degradable paper strip so all that the gardener needs to do is to lay the strip into a drill and cover it with soil. When the plants finally appear, they will be perfectly evenly spaced. Seeds are either sown in situ or are germinated in a protected environment and then planted out as more hardy seedlings.

Rather than go into the different methods on a general basis, we will start to look at some of the more commonly grown plants individually and this will give you a more practical approach that you can then use more widely. In this book, we will focus on those plants that are grown by almost all gardeners. In the next book of advanced techniques, we will delve more deeply into less common crops that add that little bit more adventure, both to the cultivation and to your dining table. It is here that the whole process starts to become a little addictive.

TOMATOES

Although not a true vegetable, we won't get bogged down in botanical classification and in this instance, we will treat them as one. Tomatoes are one of the most widely eaten vegetable crops and part of the reason for this is that they can be used for such a variety of culinary purposes. You will find them as important ingredients in everything from salads to sauces and pizzas to jams.

There is a huge variety of sizes, shapes, colours and tastes to choose from and, to be honest, most of what is on offer in the regular supermarket is merely a bland tip of a very large iceberg. Of all the vegetables that you will produce, few can match the taste of a fresh tomato picked directly from the vine and popped straight into your mouth while still warm from the sun. Tomatoes can also be expensive, so growing your own makes economic sense.

I won't even dare suggest what varieties you should choose as that would be like offering you fashion guidance having never met you. I would recommend that if you have contact with any local gardeners in your area that you ask some suggestions.

Some cultivars will do better in one area than another and I have never met a gardener who is not happy to share knowledge of this kind. Just be prepared to spend a while listening once they get started.

There are three basic forms of tomato plant. The indeterminate can grow to 2.5 meters in height. Semi-determinates are shorter and then there are bush varieties that can be as small as 25 centimetres. Taller varieties will need to be securely staked, especially if they bear large fruit like the 'Coeur de Boeuf' or the 'Beefsteak'. I would suggest growing at least three different varieties. When you place them on your planting plan be sure to take the height and size into account so that they are not casting too much shade on your other crops. In general, this would mean putting them at the northern end of your beds when growing in the northern hemisphere.

In warm climates, tomato seeds can be sown directly into the ground in drills as soon as the last frosts have passed. A drill is a gardening term for a narrow trench into which the seeds are laid before being covered with soil. Gardeners love obscure terms like this because it makes us sound far more skilled and intellectual and the term shallow trenches doesn't have the same impact. An easy way to make straight drills for your beds is to first rake it over until the soil forms a nice crumbly tilth (another highly professional term that shows you know what you are talking about). Next, cut a piece of cane the width of the interior of the bed. You press this firmly down into the soil and it leaves you a perfectly formed and straight narrow trench (drill) to drop your seeds into. Tomato seeds are small so cover them with no more than a centimetre of soil, firm it down gently and water with a fine spray. A few days later, as if by a miracle, small green leaves will start to fight their way through the soil. You will need to thin these out so that the plants are evenly spaced in accordance with whatever variety you have chosen to plant. There will be instructions as to what planting distance to use printed on the seed packet.

I prefer to start my tomatoes indoors so that I get an early head start on the season and because I am too impatient to wait for the winter to end before I start gardening. Six weeks before the last frosts, I sow seed into a seed tray or plastic ice cream box with holes poked through the bottom. (Ice cream boxes are a bit of a recurring theme and good gardening requires large scale consumption of this product). Fill the box or tray with seed or cutting compost. This is a mixture that contains little or no nutrients which can rot the seed. All it does is retain moisture and provide a substrate for the seed to root into. The seed itself contains enough energy reserves in the form of starch, to get the seedling kicked off. Sprinkle the seed onto the seed compost and then lightly cover it with a thin layer of the same compost. The easiest way to do this is to place some compost into a sieve and then shake it gently over the seed tray until the seeds are just covered.

When the plantlets produce their first set of true leaves, you can gently lift them from the seed tray and plant them into individual pots containing potting soil. Lift the plants by their leaves and not by the stems which will still be very fragile. These pots need only be small and a four to six-centimetre diameter is quite large enough. Keep the soil slightly damp and place containers on a sunny window sill or in a frost free cold frame or greenhouse. As spring draws nearer you can start placing the seedlings outdoors during the day and bringing them in again at night in a process known as hardening off. This speeds their growth and allows them to gradually adapt to their final growing conditions rather than suddenly exposing them at the last minute, which could result in losses due to shock.

By the time the first frosts have passed, the seedlings will already be about 15 to 20 centimetres high and they can be planted at the correct spacing directly into your new bed. If the plants are not of the bush variety, you will need to provide suitable stakes before you plant. You are now officially a gardener and can start wearing one of those peculiar hats that are a prerequisite of the trade. Plants should be watered weekly but do not overwater as this creates the risk of all sorts of diseases and reduces the taste. The official suggestion is that each adult plant should receive about ten litres per week. An easier approach is to stick your finger into the soil at the base of the plant and see that it is still slightly damp. If the plant is suffering water stress it will tell you by looking wilted. Learning to read the condition of your plants will eventually prove far more reliable than measuring out exact quantities of water.

I am a great believer in mulch and will go into greater detail on this subject in the next chapter. Mulch is any material laid on the soil that inhibits weed growth and helps retain water. Compost makes an excellent mulch for tomatoes as they are heavy feeders. Spread a five-centimetre layer around the base of the plants but not touching the actual stem. If mulch piles up against the base of the stem it can induce rotting. The mulch will dramatically increase moisture retention while at the same time slowly leaching nutrients down to the hungry roots.

Plants will now start to grow rapidly and taller varieties will need to be tied into their stakes regularly. Pinch out all side shoots when they are three-centimetre long and as summer draws to a close pinch out the top shoot two shoots above the topmost trusses. This will mean that the plant focuses all of its growth and nutrition on the fruit rather than on continuing to try to get taller. Fruits can be harvested when ripe, but if you live in a colder area then there may still be unripe fruit on the plant as the first frosts approach. To ensure you get all the fruit to ripen, gently bend the stems over onto some straw and cover the plants with a light horticultural fleece or clear plastic sheeting. The plant will continue to grow long enough for those last fruits to be harvested.

ONIONS

Onions are another vegetable whose value in the kitchen we sometimes fail to recognize. Onions are a simply wonderful vegetable to grow because they are a hugely versatile culinary ingredient, often being used in conjunction with tomatoes. Another really great advantage that onions bring is their longevity. Even if you grow a great deal of them, they can be stored quite easily, and a good crop could well see you right through the winter.

Onions can be grown either from seed or from sets. Sets are simply small Onions that were grown and harvested, before ripening during the previous season. Sow seed in early spring in drills to a depth of one centimetre. In a raised bed you can keep your rows about 20-centimetres apart. Planting in the ground will require greater spacing but the raised beds guarantee soil quality and ease of access for harvesting so you can tighten up a little.

Sow the seed thinly and then thin the seedlings as the leaves begin to appear. You might need to do this in stages, but ideally, you want to get to a point where each plant is about 10 centimetres from its neighbour. You may be able to keep them more closely bunched if you are growing smaller varieties. There will be a suggested planting distance on the packet. If you choose to use sets then you can plant them at their requisite spacing at the beginning of spring. Plant them to a depth where just the tips appear above the surface of the soil. Sets cost more than seed does but they give you a valuable jump start in much the same way that using seedling does. In the case of both seeds and sets, the price to return ratio is so broad that you don't really need to consider it. Even if you only get to harvest a small percentage of the crop earlier, that will more than offset the extra cost.

Once established, onions need little watering except in conditions of very dry weather. One problem you may have when using sets is that blackbirds sometimes pull them up. I am not sure why they engage in this act of horticultural vandalism but I suspect that they are convinced the set hides some edible treat. Cover them with netting until they mature a little and you will easily overcome this issue. The blackbirds may make a nuisance of themselves from time to time but they are valuable allies in the war against slugs and snails.

Before storing your crop, wait until the leaves die back naturally. The bulbs can then be lifted with a fork and they should be allowed to dry thoroughly. Usually, you can just leave them on the ground for about ten days in order to do this. If the weather is wet then hang them up indoors in netting bags of the type in which you buy oranges. Once the outside layer of skin has turned to a dry parchment they are ready to be stored. They still need to be handled with care as any bruises may lead to rotting. You can continue to store them in netting bags after cutting off the dead leaves or you can plait them using their leaves. Leave them in a cool dark place with plenty of air circulation and they should last for months.

LETTUCE

Lettuce are low growing leafy annuals that can come in a variety of colours ranging from green through to red, and which have leaves that range from smooth to indented and curly. Some cultivars form tight hearts and others have no heart at all. We are all familiar with these plants as they are an almost essential ingredient of many salads in the summer months. It is up to you to choose which variety you prefer but you might like to bear this in mind. Salad wilts quite quickly making it very difficult to store. If you go for a loose leafed variety with no heart such as 'Salad Bowl' or 'Lolo Rossa' then you can cut just enough of the outside leaves for your daily needs and leave the plant in the ground. The plant will continue to produce new leaves and in this way, you prolong the harvest period and overcome the storage problem. Another advantage is that lettuces are prone to what is known as bolting. This is a situation where they grow upwards and become bitter as they rush to produce seed. Those varieties that don't have hearts are less prone to doing this.

Lettuce plants prefer cooler weather and growing conditions of between 10 and 20°C are ideal, especially if you have cooler evenings. In cooler climates, it is possible to grow these plants in succession by sowing at two to three-week intervals so that you always have a crop ready to harvest throughout the growing season which runs from spring to late summer. You may be able to grow a longer succession of lettuce, even in warmer areas, if you place them under hoops and cover it with shade cloth. Hoops are accessories that are really easy to use in raised beds.

Sow hardy varieties in the early part of autumn. You can let these overwinter and harvest them in the spring. A plastic floating mulch thrown over the top of the plants will protect them but still allow them room to grow. A floating mulch is a perforated lightweight plastic sheeting that you lay over the plants and just tuck into the soil leaving enough room that the plants can gently lift the plastic as they grow. Sow seeds in drills between 1 and 2 centimetres deep and when the first plants appear thin them to around seven centimetres. You will need to thin them again in early spring but if you suffered any losses you can easily fill the gaps with some of the thinnings. You can also plant some of these into another bed. If you live in an area that experiences heavy snow or frost then overwintering lettuce outdoors is unlikely to be successful.

More heat resistant varieties can be sown directly in early spring. They grow quickly so they will appear in just over a week. Successive planting extends the growing period but these are hard plants to grow during the hot summer months. To further extend the growing period you can sow them in trays six weeks before the last frost and then plant them out as soon as frosts have cleared. Because these seedlings are so heat adverse, it is best to plant them out in the late afternoon and water them in so that their roots remain cool and they are not too stressed as they adjust to their new home. I am a great proponent of starting plants early indoors and then planting out the seedlings as soon as the last chance of frost has passed. This requires plenty of windowsill space or a heated greenhouse. For hardier vegetables, you can use your hoops to make a little mini greenhouse in one of your raised beds and so get a jump start when the spring arrives.

Lettuce roots should always be damp but never waterlogged. This makes a raised bed the ideal place in which to cultivate them. As with tomatoes, they will tell you if they need water by wilting and providing you have been observant, you should have time to revive them. If they do start to look a little frazzled, then just sprinkle them with water even if it is during the heat of the day. Although watering in the heat of the day is regarded as the wrong thing to do when gardening, lettuce can wilt so quickly that you can afford to break the rules in this instance. These are one plant that will benefit from some of the shade that your taller tomatoes may offer, so bear that in mind when drawing up your planting plan.

Loose leaf varieties normally take around seven weeks to harvest though if you are cutting off just a few leaves from each plant you can start doing this as soon as the leaves are large enough. Other varieties, such as the 'Crispheads' and 'Cos', which have a more structured heart need to be harvested as soon as they reach maturity. If you leave them in the ground for too long then they will bolt.

BEANS

Green beans are a crop that offer many advantages to the home gardener because they are easy to store even when there is a bumper harvest. The range of beans that you can grow is huge. Beans are divided roughly into two types, those with edible pods and those whose pods must be removed before eating. We are going to look at two types of Soft Shelled Bean, the Bush Bean and the Runner Bean, which is sometimes called a Pole Bean. Both are very happy to be cultivated in raised beds and there is just something about a neat row of well trained runner beans that makes a vegetable garden look classically ornate.

Both these types of bean are warm weather beans so don't try to sow them until you are sure that the last of the frosts is past. Unless the soil has had time to warm up a little they simply won't germinate.

Sow Bush Beans in drills at a depth of about two centimetres with rows about forty centimetres apart. This is a lot closer than with a standard bed but in the raised beds you will be able to harvest them more easily so you can afford to crowd them a little. Plant seeds fifteen centimetres apart.

They will be ready to harvest in seven to eight weeks and will go on producing for a further two to three weeks. This means that if you sow a succession of seeds every three weeks, you can extend your harvest season right up until the first frosts. They are deep rooted so don't try to grow them in containers and then plant them out as success will be minimal.

Your runner beans can grow to a height of two and a half meters so you will need to supply a structure of at least this height to support them. That support needs to last through the whole summer so it should be fairly substantial. You have any number of options to choose from including trellis or tepees made from cane. Metal reinforcing grid of the type used when pouring concrete is another possibility. You will need to support it between two poles or lean two sheets against one another in a sort of A-frame, but if you do that the beans will quickly climb it. Though it may look a little more functional than aesthetically pleasing, the beans will soon disguise this.

I favour the tepee because they are easy to install. I simply force four canes into the ground at the corners of a square and then pull the tops together and tie them to make the tepee. I can grow beans up all four faces and, placed carefully they can add an architectural element to the garden, even if it is only a temporary one. You can provide cross stays by fastening shorter pieces of cane or just with string. Plant to the same depth as bush beans, and again, at about fifteen centimetres apart.

One attractive alternative to the tepee is to create a bean tunnel by making arches between two of your raised beds. Though not permanent, these arches need to be substantial enough to carry the weight of the plants and to stay in place for the whole season. Luckily you have the raised beds to use as supports so it is usually not too difficult to cobble something together. The beans will quickly grow over these to form plant tunnels. This utilizes space that you would not normally be used but it also makes for a very unique temporary feature. The beans will hang down into the tunnel and harvesting from underneath is very easy. At the same time, the tunnel provides a wonderfully shady place to sit with a garden magazine during the summer months and, in gardening terms, this officially counts as working.

Beans freeze very quickly so if you have an excess harvest they are a crop that you can continue to eat over winter. They can also be stored in sterilized mason jars.

CARROTS

Carrots are another vegetable that most of us consume on a regular basis. They are easy to grow and are well suited to the raised bed garden. In the ground, they are sometimes impeded by the presence of stones and rocks which tends to be less of an issue with raised beds. The soil the crop is being planted into has already been worked and allows for the unimpeded growth of these root vegetables. Carrots come in a far wider range of varieties than most people are aware of. There is a colour range which includes purple, yellow and black as well, as the more familiar orange, and they come in different sizes and shapes. Finger carrots can be eaten raw in salads while still very small, and there are round carrots and really deep rooted varieties. Overall, there are plenty of different options to consider and to experiment with.

Carrots don't like to be disturbed so you should sow them directly into your bed. You do this by sowing them into drills of one centimetre deep and fifteen centimetres apart. You will need to sprinkle the fine seed as evenly as possible which is sometimes a little tricky. To overcome this problem, mix the seed with some dry building sand and sprinkle by rubbing between forefinger and thumb. This makes the spread far easier to control.

Early varieties can be sown in the spring and you can cover them with some horticultural fleece if there is a risk of frost. They will need to be thinned to around seven centimetres as they develop. As they don't like having their roots disturbed you need to be gentle doing this or you can simply cut off unwanted plants with a pair of scissors. Maincrop Carrots are sown in late spring and they need only be thinned to every four centimetres. If you carefully pull up the thinnings you will have tiny minia-ture Carrots that make a sweet addition to salads. Keep sowing main crop carrots every two to three weeks up until midsummer for an ongoing succession.

Carrots should never be allowed to dry out as this encourages them to bolt. As long as the soil they are growing in remains slightly damp you can avoid this problem. Once harvested, carrots can be plunged into a bucket of damp building sand which can be stored in a cool dark place. This will ensure that you have a ready supply of fresh carrots for most of the winter months.

Just with these few crops, you will already be in a position to have a beautiful vegetable garden and dramatically reduce the amount of fresh produce that you need to purchase. You will also be introducing a far more comprehensive range of vitamins and nutrients to your diet.

There is a wide variety of other vegetables that are easy to grow and which at the moment you may not be eating regularly. Broad Beans are very easy to produce and are one of the earliest crops to harvest. That makes them an excellent vegetable to consider as the early rewards offer both motivation and encouragement. The same can be said for Radishes. They take up very little space in a garden and come through before just about everything else. They are so easy and quick that they provide a great motivator for small kids just being introduced to the 'grow your own' way of life.

Leafy greens such as Kale, Spinach and Chard are all high in vitamins and very visually pleasing. Peas grow easily and the Flat Snap Pea varieties are delicious when tossed in a hot frying pan for a few seconds or chopped and thrown into a salad. Garlic is easy to produce and in addition to being a useful plant to have in the kitchen, they also act as a deterrent to certain pests while they are still in the garden. They make excellent companion plants to Carrots which can be attacked by Carrot fly. These pests detect the presence of Carrots by smell and the odour of growing garlic acts as a protection because it disguises their odour.

Cucumbers can be encouraged to climb up a trellis attached to one edge of your raised beds and they are another of those plants that we eat on an ongoing basis during the summer. In the next book on Advanced Raised Bed Gardening we will look in greater depth at some of these plants as well as some more unusual plants like Pak Choi, Komatsuna and Sweet Potatoes. For the moment you have enough information to get growing and once you have got to grips with the various techniques in this book the next batch of information will not seem so over-whelming. Gardening is one of those subjects where one piece of information often becomes the building block for the next and in this, we are continually learning.

Before moving on, however, we need to look at one other vegetable that plays a massive role in the western diet. That is the Potato. Potatoes are eaten so widely that it would be remiss not to pay them some attention. The problem with Potatoes is that they take up quite a lot of space and if you have limited bed space you could find yourself in a position of having to choose between growing these or some of the other crops available.

Potatoes definitely will grow in a raised bed very easily if you do have space. Potatoes are grown from what are called Seed Potatoes which are just Potatoes that were bred to produce more potatoes. To grow them in your bed you don't even really need to dig them in very much. Simply place the Potato on the surface of the bed and then shuffle it around slightly until it is virtually beneath the surface. You can place the Potatoes every thirty to forty centimetres and they can then be covered with fifteen centimetres of compost or garden soil. The plants will grow up through the soil, pushing out side shoots as they do so. These shoots are where the Potatoes will eventually grow. When the leaves are protruding to around twenty or thirty centimetres add some more soil until just the top leaves are visible. This process is called earthing up. (Another professional sounding gardening term). The process can be repeated two or three times until the plant shows signs of flowering. At each stage, the side shoots will grow into the next layer of soil that you have added and the Potatoes grow on these shoots.

For the raised bed gardener, this offers several minor problems. The first is that Potatoes will take up plenty of your precious bed space. The second is that the earth you keep piling up tends to slide out of the beds and the third is that, come harvest time, the crop needs to be dug up.

Here is a far simpler solution that is space saving and easy. You need to get four old car tyres. Any tyre fitter will have heaps of these and they are more than happy to give them away. Place one tyre in your garden on a piece of weed proof membrane. It will need to be in full sun, but other than that can be put anywhere that is convenient enough for you to get water to occasionally. Next, you fill the tyre with the same soil and compost mix that you used to fill the top layer of your beds with. Tuck the growing medium into the tyre itself and gently firm down the mix. Once full, the tyre has effectively become a large pot. You now evenly space three of your chosen seed Potatoes. Cover lightly with soil and water them in.

When the plants reach twenty to thirty centimetres in height, add another tyre and gently fill it with soil and compost so that just the top few leaves are still showing. The plants will continue to grow and send out more side shoots. When they are high enough, you can add yet another tyre. When the flowers start to appear you will know that your Potatoes are ready, though it is a good idea to dig down a little and just check what they are looking like from time to time. If you are lucky you will be able to get to a depth of four tyres before you harvest, but even just three will provide a surprisingly bountiful crop. All you then need to do is pull the stack apart and gather the Potatoes. In effect, what you have done is create another raised bed using the tyres. This method gives you a very generous crop and at the same time leaves you plenty of space in your main beds. The system is easy to manage so you can grow as many Potato stacks as you think you will be able to eat. On average you should harvest three-quarters of a bag of potatoes per stack.

Potatoes can be stored in large paper or hessian sacks in any cool dark place and, providing they are not exposed to light, they will keep for months. Brush them down to remove any earth as it is dampness that will disrupt the storage process.

Don't store them near your onions or any fruit you may be storing. These let off a gas which speeds the ageing process of the potato.

Some people feel that old tyres detract from the aesthetic appearance of the garden, but this is not necessarily true. As soon as the plants are in leaf, the appearance is perfectly acceptable and if you want to, you can go as far as painting the tyres in a colour that suits your garden design. They are also so easy to position that you can always tuck them behind a shed or elsewhere out of sight. If the tyres really offend your sense of the aesthetic then you can plant potatoes in a container such as an old barrel, bucket or even one of your Trugs. Whatever you opt for you will need to drill holes in the bottom. Though these containers are not usually as large as stacked tyres, they are portable and can be moved even when your potatoes are growing. There will be much more on container gardening in the fifth book in this series.

Now that you have a good range of vegetables growing, you might want to look at one or two other plants that will add value either to your diet or to the appearance of the garden. Herbs are always useful but are often overlooked. Many of the Mediterranean herbs such as lavender and rosemary are shrubs and though they can be incorporated into the garden design, they will be happier in the ground than in the raised beds. There are others, though, that will thrive in a raised bed environment.

The main requirements of most herbs are plenty of sun and a well drained fertile soil. The raised beds are therefore perfect. Many of the herbs will quite happily continue to thrive if you just clip off a few leaves when you need them. This allows you to have an ongoing supply of fresh herbs growing and still have plenty for your culinary use. When you see what the supermarket can charge for a few sprigs of thyme or a leaf or two of basil, then growing your own soon makes sense. If you have limited space such as a small raised bed on a balcony or patio, then herbs may be the best route both in terms of appearance and financial return.

If space is not too much of an issue, then it is worth thinking about dedicating one bed just to herbs rather than having them in several different places. As a general rule, most of the culinary herbs have similar growing requirements so having them together makes sense. Most of the herbs we eat tend to come from hot dry Mediterranean climates and it is easy to replicate this if you are doing so with just one bed containing plants with similar needs. Many are visually pleasing and produce flowers that attract beneficial insects.

Often, people tend to ignore their raised beds during the winter months but this is really a bit of a mistake. Though there are fewer crops that can be grown over this period, it is the ideal time to work on the health of your soil and thus ensure that it is in the best possible condition right at the beginning of the following season. The soil will have broken down considerably by the end of autumn and it is now that you want to fill those beds up again so that there is time for the compost and manure to break down. All of those plants you have grown will have sucked up the nutrients and winter is the time to replace it. Fill the beds till they are overflowing as the planting mix will have sunk again by the time you are ready to start replanting in the spring. This is the time to throw in plenty of farmyard manure so that it breaks down and doesn't burn your plants.

There is another way to ensure that your beds have plenty of nutrients built into them by the next season. This involves growing what is called a cover crop or green fertilizer and, though often neglected by gardeners, it is really very easy and worthwhile to do this. Some crops actually bind nitrogen into the soil and this is the macronutrient that your garden plants are most hungry for. The idea is that you sow some of these crops in autumn and then just leave them over the winter months. Two weeks before you are ready to start planting the crops for the following year you cut them down and just dig them into the beds where they will break down naturally.

While the cover crop is growing, it binds nutrients into the soil and prevents both erosion and weed build up. As it breaks down it further improves both soil texture and nutrient levels so it is an easy win-win scenario. There are many different types of plant that fill this role but the best ones are members of the leguminous family as they have the best nitrogen binding ability. These include Crimson Clover, Alfalfa, and Peas though Fall Rye and Hairy Vetch also work well.

Don't worry if you still have an autumn crop in the ground such as late Chard. Just cast the seed of your cover crop and the chard will be ready to harvest long before the cover crop can swamp it. This is a technique known as underplanting which in widely practised in agriculture.

Some cover crops produce flowers which act as an early source of food for bees and other beneficial insects. Once the flowering period is over, however, cut the plants down before they go to seed or you could find yourself with cover crop popping up all over the show over the summer months, and in places you really don't want it. A simple whiz with a lawn strimmer will make this a straightforward task. Come the spring, the green fertilizer you have dug in will have rotted down and your nutrient levels will be perfect for the start of the new growing season. Of course, gardening does not need to be restricted to the warmer months and for those that can tolerate working outdoors during the colder weather, book ten in this series will be looking specifically at that subject.

START GROWING – RECAP:

- Decide on what crops you are most likely to eat. Use your shopping list as a guide

- Always keep a diary and records as this will prove invaluable in later years
- Choose between seed or seedlings. They both have advantages
- Growing tips for the more commonly eaten vegetables
- Consider at least some herbs
- Tyre potatoes offer space and labour saving possibilities

6

WATERING, FERTILIZERS AND PEST CONTROL

*I*n this chapter, we will be looking at three fundamental aspects of gardening that people often tend to overlook. Sowing and propagating tend to hog the limelight on the vegetable gardening stage. There is so much pleasure to be had from watching seeds emerge from their coatings and spreading those first delicate leaves, or the early green shoots forcing their way through the soil in a tyre planted with seed potatoes that the more routine stuff can seem a little lacklustre.

It is the routine chores that will make the difference between a successful crop and failure. All three of the subjects that we will be examining in this chapter play a crucial role in the garden. Their importance is augmented by the fact that you have chosen to garden in an environmentally responsible manner. When you choose to go organic you take a moral stand, and sometimes in life when we do that, we make things a little harder for ourselves. That is certainly the case when gardening without chemicals. You are no longer able to simply toss a handful of fertilizer over the bed and allow chemistry to supply the nutrients. Pest control ceases to be simply a matter of reaching for a spray bottle and annihilating an entire swathe of insects with just a few short squirts.

There are few areas in gardening that have been as contentiously debated as this one in recent years. There can be no doubt that when we decide to set aside the lethal insecticides and industrial fertilizers, we add an element of difficulty to our lives. I won't try to sugar coat that fact. More effort is required and yields will very often decrease, certainly in the short term. To counter that, however, the organic gardener can comfort himself with the knowledge that his crops do not contain toxic residues, he is not contaminating underground water supplies and he is not contributing to the massive decline in insect and wildlife populations that we have witnessed over the last few decades.

The benefits of the organic garden tend to be seen over a more extended period of time. The rewards are more nuanced and gentler than they are when you allow the big pharmaceutical companies to participate in your gardening endeavours. Gradually, over time, you will start to notice a change. That change will become more obvious as your eye becomes accustomed to seeing what benefits nature has to offer if we allow her the time to work her magic.

In the garden where pesticides are used, all insects become the enemy. There is no difference between a beneficial insect and one that will attack the crops, no innocent civilian or neutral bystander. The chemicals we apply do not discriminate. What is the point of being able to identify the aphid eating larvae of a ladybird when it is going to be killed by the toxic mist that you blast the crops with. The organic gardener needs to become something of a cross between an entomologist and a soil scientist. Instead of just viewing his raised beds as a garden, the organic gardener needs to see the whole area as a small ecosystem. One in which he plays a large hand in managing. Over time, the organic garden evolves into a mini oasis, where insects thrive and the soil is rich. As if by miracle, birds will start to make an appearance and they will soon be followed by frogs, toads, newts and array of other creatures, many of whom will assist the gardener in the constant battle against snails, slugs and caterpillars.

Now that your beds are filled with soil that is rich in microorganisms and humus, and your crops are starting to make their first appearance, it is time to really ensure that your water usage is as efficient and well managed as possible. Unless you have a lawn of exotic grass blends, the vegetable garden is the area of the garden where most water is required and thus, where most water management needs to take place. Bear in mind that a single lettuce requires seventy litres of water to reach maturity. There's a shocking figure for you.

I mentioned earlier in this book that I would be revisiting the subject of mulch. This is an area that is very often ignored and one that I am passionate about. It is so easy to do, normally free and so good for the garden that I can never understand why people don't use mulch far more widely. It is crucial to retaining moisture, boosting soil condition and, of course, slowing down the rate of evaporation. At the same time, it smothers weeds and saves the gardener effort. On top of all that it is often free. What is there not to be passionate about?

Mulch can be any material that covers the soil surface and retains moisture. In decorative gardens, people often use visually pleasing mulches such as pebbles, broken slates or coloured wood chips. In the vegetable garden, I require more from a mulch than that it merely be pleasing to the eye. I want the mulch to be an organic material that will breakdown to add to my already healthy soil and there are many options to choose from. In keeping with true self sufficient tradition, I like the product I use to be homemade and cost nothing.

My preferred choice of mulch is always compost. As you first start gardening, you may only have a limited amount of your own compost available, but don't worry. This is one product that you will soon be producing plenty of. I like to lay it about six centimetres deep all across the surface of my beds, leaving small wells around the stem of each plant. Over time the compost will break down and become incorporated into the soil and our colleagues, the earthworms, love to drag it down and reduce my tilling at the end of the season. In the next book on advanced raised bed gardening, we will look more deeply at making compost, but although people have written realms on the subject, it really is very easy. Basically, compost is just broken down vegetable matter such as lawn clippings, leaves and all of those non-woody bits and pieces that the act of gardening, and cooking, produce on a constant and ongoing basis. This is then mixed with soil or manure and allowed to break down naturally to form a rich dark crumbly material.

If you have any deciduous trees in your garden, then leaves will be one product that you acquire plenty of come the fall. Before becoming a gardener, you may have seen these fallen leaves as a nuisance. Now they become what organic gardeners refer to as black gold. Instead of burning them and pumping clouds of smoke into the environment, just heap them into a corner where they will break down into black crumbly leaf mould which is great to mulch with. Leaf mould is suitable for retaining moisture and adding texture but it does not have the nutrients that compost does. As the leaves break down, I mix them with farmyard manure and that breaks them down further and turns them into a sort of compost which in turn addresses the lack of nutrient problem.

Lawn clippings are very easy to get hold of even if you don't have a lawn of your own. I like to let them break down for a month before using them on beds that have vegetables growing in them, but they always make good mulch and soil conditioner after that. When you apply it you will be amazed at how much water they retain and how quickly they break down and get absorbed into the soil.

In your first season of gardening, you may not have easy access to any of the above mulches but there are still plenty of free options. Straw is cheap, light and makes an excellent mulch. At the end of the season, you can just dig it into the beds and let it break down naturally. Most tree surgeons and timber yards will let you have as many wood chips as you like and even shredded newspaper will do a good job of retaining moisture.

The mulch will act as a sort of blotting paper and prevent the top layer of soil from forming a crust off which water can simply run away. Once you have mulched your soil and are sure that texture is not an issue, then when you water is the next factor to take into account. A simple test of whether your beds are damp enough is to stick your finger into the soil. The top inch should be dry and after that, it should be damp but not waterlogged. It is better to water deeply and less often than to do lots of shallow watering. This encourages the root system of your plant to grow more deeply and thus it will be better equipped to overcome any dry spells. A deep rooted plant also accesses nutrients more effectively thus producing healthier and more tasty crops.

As a rule of thumb, the best time of day to water is the early morning or late afternoon. This cuts down on evaporation and allows the water to sink further into your soil. If your plants suddenly start to wilt then feel free to break this rule, but you will need to examine why they suddenly became water stressed. A healthy plant growing in a well conditioned soil should not need to be watered in the middle of the day and perhaps your mulch has become too thin or the previous watering was not deep enough. Don't water every day unless you have to. If the lower layer of soil is damp, then skip the watering until the following day. Weather conditions will obviously play a part in how much evaporation takes place. If it rains lightly, never assume that you don't need to water. Sometimes a drizzle is not enough to permeate the soil effectively. Just stick your finger into the ground an hour after the rain stops and see if it is still damp.

How you water is another factor to take into consideration. Simply turning on a sprinkler and allowing water to go everywhere is probably one of the least effective methods of applying water. It may be labour saving but this system is a far from an ideal solution. Not only will some of the water evaporate before hitting the ground, but it will also land in places where water is not required such as on paths. Wet leaves can add to the risk of moulds, blights and funguses and that can easily be avoided using less random watering techniques. Using a watering can with a fine rose on it eliminates the problem of poorly targeted water but ceases to be viable where you have several beds. In that case, a wand attached to a garden hose allows you to water at the base of your plants which is exactly where you want it. If you buy a wand that only applies water when you pull a trigger that further increases effective water control.

Stepping up from the hose or can is the irrigation system. There was a time when irrigation systems were quite complicated and remained the domain of the irrigation expert. Today, systems are far easier to assemble and install and there is no need to pay for outside expertise. You can even buy battery operated timers that simply fit onto a standard garden tap and can be set to water the garden at a time, or times, of your choosing. The price is very reasonable and if you can set an alarm clock you can set a basic irrigation timer.

The irrigation comes in two basic forms. The first is a hose which you run through your beds and into which you plug either drippers or spray nozzles. I would suggest you avoid the spray system for the reasons we have just mentioned. The drippers work well but will need to be run to the base of each plant that needs to be watered. This can result in a complicated network of small pipes that are very easy to pierce during routine gardening options. I talk as someone who has some experience in this regard. The drip lines may seem neat and logical as you set them among your fledgling plants. As the garden develops and leaves start to flourish, all logic and preplanning seems to vanish and you have no idea where the drip lines go. That said, in plants that are less randomly placed such as tomatoes, there is still a place for drip feeders.

Another system is the leaky pipe system, and these too come in different versions. Both systems have a pipe that is run through the bed. One allows water to seep through it at any point as the pipe sweats. The other has a series of fine holes all along its length out of which the water can escape into the soil. In my experience, the sweat pipes have a shorter life span than those that are perforated. Both systems can be connected with simple joints and elbows to allow you to run the pipes up and down the length of the beds as you deem appropriate. They can be pinned in place with simple wire staples that you can make yourself.

All of the above options require the gardener to do a few experiments. You will need to figure out how far from the pipe the water spreads and for how long the tap must run to supply sufficient water to all parts of the bed. Whatever kit you opt for, it will usually come with a set of instructions as to the width and depth of spread. I suggest you use this as a guideline but still do your own experiments. In general, a leaky pipe system will supply sufficient water to reach around thirty centimetres from each side of the pipe. For a four foot wide bed, you will need to run two lengths up each bed which is easy to do.

Irrigation systems, especially those that are timer controlled, can save the gardener a great deal of time and allow for holidays and away weekends. They are not fool proof, however, and all joints and connections need to be checked regularly. They are being put under fluctuating pressure from the water on an ongoing basis and if one of them pops open, you will end up with lots of water at the broken joint and none throughout the rest of the system. You can strengthen each joint by binding it closed with thin wire.

The other thing that all gardeners should consider is a water capture system. Even the small roof of a garden shed is enough to capture substantial amounts of water when fitted with gutters that lead to some sort of water butt. If all the rainwater that runs off an average house is captured then a gardener should never need to access mains water. Of course, even if you capture water, there is the question of how you then get it to where you want it. These days it is easy to purchase a small pump that will easily and efficiently transport your free water to your beds. Electric pumps come in two types. One is submersible and the whole pump is then dropped into the water reservoir and a hose leading from it carries water to the garden. The other has a hose that sucks the water from the butt to the pump and then it is pumped into the watering hose. Both options are easy to use and you will soon recuperate their cost in reduced water bills.

Things become a little more complicated if you do not have an electrical socket in a place that allows you to plug your pump into the electricity supply. All is not lost, however. It is easy to purchase a small pump that runs on either petrol or diesel fuel. These days, fuel pumps can be amazingly small and light and are easily lifted by even the least physical of gardeners. Before purchasing such an item, check with the supplier to ensure that the pump that you choose can push the water from your butts to your beds.

FERTILIZING RAISED BEDS

Because you have opted to be an organic producer, you have taken away the option of just tossing a few handfuls of chemicals onto your beds to supply the nutritional needs of your vegetables. That certainly doesn't need to detract in any way from the quality of your produce and there are many ways of supplying your plants with food that don't involve the participation of large chemical companies. The first and most important issue is to ensure that your growing medium is of the highest possible quality. I have already mentioned this on several occasions and by now you will know how to do this. I apologize if I seem to bang on the drum of soil quality too often, but it really is the foundation of all good gardening.

Once your soil is in optimum condition, you will then need to keep it that way by adding nutritious natural mulches two or three times during the growing season. The plants will be grabbing nutrients as fast as they can and you will need to supplement what is in the soil to replace what the plants absorb. When you prepare the beds you can augment their nutrient levels by adding slow release natural fertilizers such as bone meal, hoof and horn meal or fish and blood meal. Because these are slow release fertilizers there is little that you can actually do wrong with them and they will not burn even the most tender of plants. You don't even need to dig them in if you don't want to. Before planting just sprinkle a handful per square yard and that fertilizer will slowly break down over the season. These products are very inexpensive but there is some cost and so here is a free alternative.

Plants like Stinging Nettles, Comfrey and Yarrow are known as dynamic accumulators. They have deep root systems and they suck up the nutrients from the soil in which they are grown. The nutrients then become trapped in the leaves. By making them into a liquid we get a homemade fertilizer known as fertilizer tea. This can be diluted with water and poured at the base of your plants every week or two. This ensures high nutrient levels no matter how much the growing vegetables absorb. These teas are perfect for heavy feeders such as Peppers, Cucumbers and Tomatoes.

It is a good idea always to have a bunch of Comfrey growing in the corner of your garden. The plant is prized by herbalists who have been using it to heal wounds and broken bones for centuries. It is a hardy perennial and you can cut it back and harvest the large hairy leaves as often as four times a year. If the plant is established it will soon grow back with renewed vigour. The flowers are favoured by bees and other beneficial insects and, frozen into ice cubes, they add an interesting decorative element to summer drinks or sprinkled on salads.

Yarrow is equally undemanding and stinging nettles are one plant that you should have no trouble getting hold of. You will need a large dustbin or barrel with a fitted lid. Now you simply cut down the plant or plants, you are using and fill the bottom half of your container. Don't get hung up with quantities and percentages as so many articles and magazines suggest. Simply cram half the container with whatever of the three plants is easiest to come by, preferably a mixture of all three, and top up with water.

Some people like to weigh the leaves down with a brick or a rock but not only is this unnecessary, I advise against it for reasons that will become obvious. Now all you need to do is stir the mix every day or two. Gradually, as it matures, the water will turn dark and a noxious looking grey sludge will appear on the surface between stirrings. Don't be alarmed by this. It merely means that your magic potion is progressing well. A word of caution here - the mix smells really bad, especially if it contains a high proportion of nettles. Gardeners become some-what accustomed to working with materials that may not be deemed sweet smelling by the less educated population. This one really is noteworthy, however. If you spill some on yourself it is capable of testing even the strongest of marriages, which is why I don't weigh mine down with a brick. I don't want to have to fish that brick out before I can use the mix and risk expensive divorce litigation in the process.

After three to five weeks, your mix is ready for use and you can carefully tip it into plastic containers such as large milk or fruit juice bottles. It will store in a dark room for up to a year. To apply it, you must first dilute it with water at a ratio of four to one and if you want to use it on smaller seedlings you should increase that ratio to eight to one. You can now water the base of each plant with the homemade fertilizer once a week and you are assured of a nutrient rich growing mix.

There will be a green to black mass of unidentifiable plant material left in the bottom of the barrel and this can now be poured onto the compost heap before starting the next mix. Over time you will reach a point where you just always have a barrel of this tea quietly brewing away in some shady corner of the garden. You will then have a constant supply of liquid fertilizer and there is no need to buy a chemical equivalent. You can feed your plants safe in the knowledge that you are not polluting the groundwater or poisoning the kids.

For an even more powerful concoction, fill a fabric bag such as a pillowcase with chicken manure and leave that hanging in a barrel of water for a month to six weeks. Chicken manure is really high in nitrogen which is the macronutrient that plants need most of. Used directly on the garden it can quickly burn plants, especially young and tender ones. If it is made into a manure tea like this, it can be diluted with water to a ratio of ten to one and you will have your own high nitrogen fertilizer that costs nothing. Once again, the smell is a little on the obnoxious side so handle with care and long rubber gloves.

PEST CONTROL

Ever since humankind started growing food we have had to compete with an array of pests. Some crops will be unaffected by one pest but will be vulnerable to another. Colorado Beetles, for example, love to eat Potatoes while Lettuce is the Caviar of the Slug and Snail community. Getting to know what pests to expect on what vegetables is a matter of experience, but all prevention is aided by close observation. Pests don't tend to just sit out in the open and make life easy for the gardener. They are sneaky little devils and they hide with as much cunning and expertise as the best trained guerrilla fighter. The first defence is always going to be a keen sense of observation. Look at the plant for signs of stress, nibbled leaves or hidden eggs. You will need to look under leaves and just below the soil surface carefully.

You also need to learn who your allies are. Ladybirds and their larvae are ferocious hunters of Aphids. The Blackbird and the Thrush both delight in Snails and Slugs. Even the tiny Blue and Great Tits become carnivores during the nesting season. An adult bird will bring between 700 and 1000 Caterpillars to its chicks per day. That is a phenomenal amount and if that is what they need to feed their young, then you can only imagine how devastating the widespread use of pesticides must be to the bird population. As you abandon the use of pesticides in your garden you will witness an increased number of these allies taking up residence nearby. It is one of the most soul warming aspects of gardening. Gradually you reach a natural equilibrium in which the beneficial creatures keep down the pests to a degree where a healthy status quo is reached. That equilibrium is what the organic gardener hopes to achieve. Those that are not environmentally friendly must attempt to annihilate all competition using chemicals and, in so doing, destroy the beneficial creatures in the process. In effect, they must produce an arena that is perfect for their crops but a toxic desert for anything else. The organic gardener takes a far wider view.

Once you develop your eye and learn to spot insects, teach yourself to identify them. Ladybirds and Praying Mantises are a great asset in your garden and there are many others. You can either purchase a book on insects or a book on garden pests. Both will help you differentiate friend from foe. On the internet, you can purchase beneficial insects that will quickly colonize any healthy new environment into which they are released. Even large scale commercial growers are now starting to see the advantage of using bio bugs to attack pests. These come in the form of predatory wasps, mites and flies which thrive on pests that might attack your plants. You can purchase them from breeders and then release them into your garden.

After observation skills, the next vital factor to consider is that insects will always attack weakened and diseased plants over healthy ones. Because you have prepared your soil and fed your plants so well, you have already put yourself at an advantage. Healthy plants are able to resist attack more efficiently and are better able to survive even when attacked. If you see plants that are looking weak or sickly, it might be a good idea to remove them rather than hoping they will limp back to good health. A fragile plant can act as a beachhead from which pests can launch attacks on neighbouring plants. Planting crops at the correct time also helps them to get established as they are not fighting their natural tendencies. They are quicker to get established and move beyond that vulnerable seedling stage more rapidly.

Another factor that works to the organic gardener's advantage is that we grow a wide variety of crops. Commercial growers tend to focus on just one or two crops and this, in turn, leads to the development of insect communities that thrive on that particular crop. By having a range of crops we prevent the build up of any one type of pest. Even when we do come under attack in one area, there are other plants that will remain pest free so that we still have a harvest.

Harvesting early is a defence mechanism that many gardeners overlook. Just as we like to eat our produce when it is perfectly ripe, the pests often have similar in tastes. Many fruit and vegetables will ripen perfectly well if picked just prior to ripening and then will continue to ripen when stored in an insect free environment.

Companion planting is another area that can bring huge benefits and we will be looking at this subject in some depth in book three of the series. Plants like onion, garlic, and even flowering plants like marigolds, have specific smells that either hide the presence of crops that pests favour or discourage the pest altogether.

There is no denying that when you choose to grow without the use of pesticides you are going to lose a certain amount of your produce to pests. That can be offset against the fact that in your raised bed you can grow a higher proportion of crops than you may normally have done elsewhere.

Despite all of the methods we have just looked at, there is no denying that suffering crop losses to thieving bugs and insects can be disheartening. Even the most organic gardener does not like to rely entirely on defensive methods. Sometimes you need to go on the offensive. Keen observation will help you spot your enemy and very often, in the case of Caterpillars and bugs, they can be removed and destroyed physically. Even the most faint hearted of gardeners can become quite aggressive if their vegetables are in danger. You will soon find yourself ruthlessly crushing beetles underfoot and picking off Caterpillars to feed to the Chickens in a sort of gladiatorial blood bath.

On the subject of chickens, these birds are voracious hunters of garden pests. When they are scratching away at the soil they are doing so to unearth creatures that would almost definitely be competitors for your vegetables. Chickens are a great asset towards pest control but only when you don't have a crop or they will quickly either want to share it with you or damage it with their digging. Letting them into the raised bed garden for a few hours each day while you prepare your beds is a good strategy but only if you are sure that you can keep them out later in the year. Ducks, on the other hand, are far less inclined to damage or eat your harvest but are experts at spotting snails and slugs.

Finally, there are non chemical pesticides. Many are available commercially but here are a couple that you can make yourself. My favourite is vegetable soap. This product can be sprayed onto any plants and will make them unpleasant to eat. When you have an invasion of Aphids, a spray bottle of this soap mixed with water will blast them away very effectively. Look out for Ants as these creatures farm the Aphids by moving them to the most tender shoots and leaves. The aphid produces a sticky liquid called honeydew and the Ants then eat this. If you spot Ants on the leaves of your plants then pay attention because it is almost certain that they are there in the company of their carefully managed Aphid flock. You can blast the aphids with the soapy mixture and they will get blasted off or simply slide away. Because the product is just soapy water you can augment this by rubbing the leaf between your fingers as you spray.

Unlike a chemical spray, there are no toxins that are going to kill other creatures or poison your produce. You need to be aware, however, that this is a short term solution and you will need to spray regularly or the pests will return. I carry a spray bottle with me and use it liberally against Aphids, Caterpillars and Shield bugs. You can get away with a strong concentration of dishwashing liquid and it will have a similar effect though, because it is thinner, it tends not to cling to the leaves as effectively.

To augment the power of your liquid soap you can boost it with crushed Garlic, Chillies or even a Nicotine solution made from soaking cigarettes in water for a few days. These all just add to the unsavoury effect that you are trying to create, though I find straight vegetable soap solution perfectly adequate.

When on the subject of building beds, I mentioned that it was possible to install physical barriers such as wire grills to stop moles and netting attached to the beds to discourage rabbits and deer. If you really have a significant invasion of insect pests, then there is no reason that you should not net off your beds with fine netting to prevent their access altogether. The raised beds facilitate this because it is so easy to attach either hoops or posts onto which the netting can be attached. Although it is comforting to have this option, I have never found it to be necessary because the raised beds provide such an ideal growing environment for my crops. They seem to quickly establish themselves and outgrow that stage where they are most vulnerable.

There will never be a time when the gardener can ever let his or her guard down entirely. Eventually, that all important observation skill simply becomes second nature and whenever you are watering, weeding or just wandering through the beds at the end of the day, you will find yourself turning leaves over and looking beneath the plants. As the environment starts to regain its natural equilibrium, you will begin to see a comforting amount of predatory insects and fewer pests. The bird population will increase and the soil will become a haven for worms. That is when you will know that you have really made a positive change to that tiny natural habitat that you have created.

PESTICIDES, FERTILIZERS AND WATERING – RECAP:

- A touch of the organic debate
- The magic of mulch
- Fertilizer teas
- The power of observation
- Predators and pest
- Good water management
- Irrigation options

7

COMMON MISTAKES AND
CHALLENGES

*B*y now you will have gathered that I am a big fan of raised beds but it would be remiss of me to pretend that they are the fix all answer to gardening. In this chapter, I intend to go over some of the most common mistakes that new raised bed gardeners make as well as a few things that might make you want to consider other options such as planting directly into the ground. Most of the problems we will be looking at have relatively straightforward solutions, but at least you will have the whole picture and be able to make a realistic assessment of which route will work best for you.

First and foremost, there are the start-up costs. When you garden in open ground you prepare your soil and away you go. Raised beds require you to spend money before you can even get a crop into the ground. If you are lucky, you may be able to recycle materials, but the weight of soil puts pressure on the beds and those cobbled together with old doors and pallets are going to have a relatively short life span. As we don't like to use pressure treated wood because of the chemicals they contain, all wooden beds will eventually degrade. If you are using regular pine scaffold boards then you should not expect a life span of more than five years from each raised bed. Red cedar and some other types of wood will last longer, but even they are not a forever remedy. Some materials such as brick, stone and corrugated iron may indeed last for decades but the initial cost of their installation needs to be taken into account.

Raised beds require a lot of good quality soil to fill them in the first place and this can add to the initial outlay. This then needs to be mixed with garden compost and other more nutritious Ameliorants and, as you are just starting out, you probably have not built up your own supply and will need to buy some in.

Raised beds take time to build. They also need more forward planning than merely planting in the open. All of us, when starting a new project, are anxious to get going, but with raised beds, there is an awful lot of preparation work to do before we get to that delightful planting stage. If we don't plan the positioning properly or we put the beds together poorly, we will be punished at a later stage. Beds must be orientated correctly to take advantage of the movement of the sun and the preplanning is critical to ensure we have wide enough paths and access to things like water and compost.

If you are a fan of machinery such as rotavators, they can be more difficult to use in raised beds because you will need to lift the machine into the beds and then use it in a fairly confined space. Even when digging with just a fork or spade, you need to take care not to use the frame for leverage as this could cause damage. In my experience, there is less digging involved with raised beds and there is now a lot of research that suggests that excessive working of the soil can damage its microorganism population and its water carrying capacity.

Tall plants in high beds mean that some crops such as runner beans and taller varieties of tomato are that much higher than they would be if planted at ground level. For the shorter gardener, this could become an issue during harvest or when tying into frames and trellises.

Despite all of these issues, I still think that raised beds are something that most gardeners should consider. Now we will look at some of the most common mistakes that gardeners make when starting out with raised beds.

Many of the most common mistakes are made at the planning stage. Placing the beds too far from a water supply or orientating them incorrectly are the most frequently seen issues. If you design your beds too wide, then you will need to walk on them to get to the plants in the middle. This will quickly lead to soil compaction and eliminate one of the major advantages of the raised bed – accessibility. Keep beds to a maximum width of four feet unless you are seven feet tall or have arms the length of a Neanderthal. Next is making paths too small which is why I usually recommend keeping them as wide as a wheelbarrow with just a little bit extra so that the gardener can slide around the barrow without having to walk all the way around the bed. That said, there are plenty of instances where this rule would simply not be viable. With more and more people going down the urban farmer route, there is often a need to use as much growing space as possible. If this is your intention, then cut your paths to a width that you can walk down but be sure to consider that full grown plants will overlap the edge of their beds.

Raised beds can dry out faster than open beds, particularly if the soil does not contain enough humus. This will be most notice-able where the soil and the walls of the bed meet. If the soil becomes too dry it will contract and a gap will appear down which water will simply flow away. Two things will prevent this from becoming a problem. One is to ensure that the soil contains plenty of absorbent matter such as compost and the other is straight forward observation. If you are paying atten-tion to your beds you will be able to resolve this long before it can become an issue.

A problem that is very rare with raised beds is that they become waterlogged. This will only occur if the underlying earth is very heavy with clay, or if there is a compacted layer beneath the original soil surface. Very occasionally this can occur if heavy machinery has passed over an area and compacted the subsoil to such a degree that drainage becomes impossible. If you encounter this problem, the short term solution is to dig small drainage trenches from the base of the frame. This will allow any water that is getting trapped to escape and you should be able to see out the season in this way. As soon as the season is over you will need to address the problem on a more permanent basis. Unfortunately, this will entail unpacking all of the growing medium from within the frame and then digging down until you break through the layer beneath that is causing the issue. After that the bed can be filled again. It is hard work but fortunately, it is also very uncommon. Usually when constructing the frames you pre dig the soil on which they will be positioned and this would alert you to any underlying issues.

Raised beds can be hotter in the summer months and colder in the winter. Obviously, a bed that is exposed to the sun on the sides and the surface will become warmer. In general, most vegetable crops will benefit from the extra heat. If you are planning on growing crops that have heat sensitive roots you may have to consider this but it is easily resolved with a little extra watering which will soon cool everything down. Another possibility is to install shade netting and this is something that gardeners in warmer regions such as South Africa and Australia are turning to more and more as the climate changes. The fact that you are using raised beds won't really make much difference and if anything, they offer an easy way to attach posts for supporting the shade netting itself.

In cooler regions where freezing takes place, then the cold comes into play. Generally, in these regions, the gardener is growing a hardy crop or a cover crop to turn into green manure the following spring. Here too, the temperature difference in a raised bed shouldn't affect your decision that much.

When planting crops there are other factors that the newer gardener sometimes forgets to take into account. Taller crops should be grown on the northern ends of the beds when growing in the northern hemisphere where the sun will be to the south. This stops them casting too much shade on smaller plants. The opposite applies in the southern hemisphere. The raised bed gardener will generally plant more densely than the open ground gardener. There are two reasons for this. The first is that raised beds often have a limited planting area and the gardener naturally wants to get as much of a harvest as he can from the limited space available. The second is that the more intensely managed growing medium simply allows the gardener to plant more crops and so therefore, why not?

When it comes to planting, one of the commonest errors, and this certainly is not restricted to new gardeners, is to forget to label the plant or seed that is going into the bed. It is easy to focus on the primary objective, which is planting and watering in, and then to forget what seems like a minor detail. If you have just spent an hour planting Tomato seedlings called Super Sweet it can't be that hard to remember, surely? The next day you plant Cherokee Purple and the day after that you pop in a couple called Early Girl. None of these are particularly difficult names to recall – at least in the short term. Come back a few weeks later, and unless you have been a particularly successful contender on the television show Mastermind, it is highly unlikely you will not know one plant from another. Add to that a few types of carrot, some bean varieties and some unidentified plants you scored from a neighbour, and your garden soon becomes a jigsaw puzzle which you will never be able to repeat, even if everything grows perfectly.

Record keeping is critical, and I dealt earlier with garden plans and the importance of a diary. It starts here with the planting. Every row of different plants needs to be labelled and dated. This allows you to see what plants perform best and to show off to any visitors as you casually throw out names and cultivars as you wander between the beds. Plant labels can be as simple as a lolly stick with the details written in indelible ink, or as ornate as individually cut pieces of slate or copper dangled from delicately twisted wire stands.

One other common error is to assume that once you have harvested all that is in the beds, all work is over until the following spring. If you just leave your soil bare over the winter months, many of the nutrients that the plants need will be leached out of it by the start of spring. It doesn't take long to cast some seed for a winter cover crop or to heap a rich mulch over the surface. When the spring comes, your associates the worms will have dragged much of the mulch deep into the soil. If the soil is left bare many of them will die along with billions of the other microorganisms that go into making a healthy soil.

The final, often repeated mistake is to not pay enough attention to your beds during the growing period. Even in inclement weather, you would do well to check on your plants every single day. They are living things, after all, and they depend on the gardener for their well being. This is important in both raised and open ground beds. By paying attention and re-staking early, a plant that has toppled over could well be a saved. Spotting a few caterpillars and crushing them along with any nearby eggs can make a huge difference over a twenty-four hour period.

The time lapse between a few nibbled leaves and a seriously devoured plant can be remarkably short.

TACKLING MISTAKES AND CHALLENGES – RECAP:

- Failure to plan ahead can be disastrous
- Labelling and record keeping are critical
- The soil must be taken seriously
- You should use cover crops or mulch over winter

CONCLUSION

This book on raised bed gardening is the first of a series of books designed to lead the reader gently through the process of gardening in all its many different aspects. My objective in writing this series was to share the knowledge that I have gained over the years, but also to stimulate passion. Gardening is not merely a science or a collection of different techniques. It is also an art form, a therapy and a hobby that can become horribly addictive.

For some time I gardened using chemical pesticides and fertilizers. When I first became a gardener that was just what people did and anyone going down the organic route was considered a little bit of a fanatic. Over time I came to see that what the 'green fringe' was preaching was true. They were harvesting a yield that was comparable to mine but they could rest in the assurance that they were not harming the environment or themselves as they carried out their work. As I researched more widely, I reached a point where I could no longer keep pretending to myself that that was the case in my own garden. Scandal after scandal revealed instances in which the agrochemical industry either twisted the truth or abandoned it altogether to sell their chemicals.

It is hard to be a gardener without inadvertently becoming an environmentalist. Plants are a part of nature, after all, just as are we. To nurture a plant is to work hand in hand with nature. The more I delved into the world of chemical free gardening, the more it became obvious to me that it was not only a viable option, it was the only option if I was going to be true to myself. Although this series has followed an organic route, it is clearly not the only route and each gardener will have to decide for himself what principals to adhere to and which ones to set aside.

This book will have provided readers with enough information to get started as a raised bed gardeners. Although it only scratches the tip of the iceberg, for some it will contain all the information they ever need to fulfil all of their gardening ambitions. They will have learned how to make and position beds, how to fill them and how to maintain them. They also have enough information to produce some of the most commonly consumed vegetables, deal with the most frequently confronted challenges and care for the beds so that they are ready to produce another crop as soon as the next season allows them to.

We humans are not a species that is always easily satisfied. For many, the desire to take their gardening to the next level will become overwhelming, which is why I have written these books as a series rather than one large volume. If a reader manages to control the gardening addiction (highly unlikely), then this book will be all that they need. They will not have been forced to payout for information they will never use. On the other hand, if a gardener wants to build on the information in this book, they can simply opt for the more advanced follow up and they will have a whole battery of new plants and techniques to experiment with.

At whatever level a gardener decides to pursue this type of gardening, raised beds are just such a practical way to grow plants. The beds can be made at a size that will provide the vegetable needs for a whole family, or small enough to sit on the balcony of a tiny apartment. When placed on legs or built high enough, this method allows people who struggle to bend or who are partially immobilized, to continue to profit from the immense pleasure of growing plants for themselves. At both ends of that spectrum, the enjoyment and self-satisfaction can be immense. Whether it is growing large quantities of vegetables, or just a handful of herbs and ornamental plants, raised bed gardening offers the gardener a method that is both practical and attainable.

Month	General	Tomatoes	Onions	Beans	Potato	Radishes	Carrots	Lettuce
Jan	Dig in cover crops or mulch heavily							
Feb								
March		Sow in pots indoors	Sow seeds or plant sets		2nd half plant seed potatoes	Sow in drills		Sow first seed
April		1st half harden off	Thin seedlings	1st half sow in pots	Earth up	1st half 2nd sowing / 2nd half / harvest	1st half 2nd sow / 2nd half sow and thin	1st half sow + thin / 2nd half Thin
May		2nd half plant out / Water and liquid feed		2nd half plant out / Sow in pots	Earth up and liquid feed	1st half / Sow again / 2nd half harvest	1st half sow / 2nd half sow and thin / Feed weekly	1st half sow + thin / 2nd half thin
June		Water and liquid feed		1st half plant out + stake / 2nd half Harvest	1st half liquid feed / 2nd half	Harvest	Keep thinning where necessary / Feed weekly	1st half / Sow
July		Water and liquid feed		Harvest	Harvest earlies / liquid feed and bone blood and fish meal	Harvest	Feed weekly / Start harvesting	2nd half harvest / Harvest
August		Water and liquid feed	Harvest and dry	Harvest	Liquid feed main crop		Continue to harvest / Feed weekly	Harvest
Sept		Harvest	Harvest and dry	Harvest	Harvest main crop		Continue to harvest / Feed weekly	
Oct	Sow cover crops	Harvest	Harvest and dry / Store excess		Store main crop			
Nov								
Dec								

Thank you for reading my book. If you have enjoyed reading it perhaps you would like to leave a star rating and a review for me on Amazon? It really helps support writers like myself create more books. You can leave a review for me by scanning the QR code below:

Thank you so much.

Peter Shepperd

ADVANCED RAISED BED GARDENING GUIDE

EXPERT TIPS TO OPTIMIZE YOUR YIELD, GROW
HEALTHY PLANTS AND TAKE YOUR RAISED BED
GARDEN TO THE NEXT LEVEL

THIS CHECKLIST INCLUDES:

- 10 items you will need to maintain your green fingered adventure.
- The highest quality Gardening items.
- Where you can buy these items for the lowest price.

The last thing we want is for your gardening project start to be delayed because you weren't prepared.

To receive your essential tool checklist, visit the link:

INTRODUCTION

"Gardens are not made by singing 'Oh, how beautiful,'
and sitting in the shade."

— RUDYARD KIPLING

This is the second in a series of ten books designed to help guide
the reader along the gently winding path from novice to compe-
tent gardener. The first book called Introduction to Raised bed
Gardening was a bit of a cheat. Not that the information it
contained was not pertinent or achievable, but precisely for the
opposite reason. I knew that once you had discovered the plea-
sures of growing your first few plants and vegetables, it was
doubtful that you would not want to expand on that knowledge.

Gardening is like that. You cautiously dip your toe in the water, and the next thing you know you want to tear your clothes off and swim naked through the vast sea of information the subject has to offer.

This book is designed to build on your existing skillset but never at a pace that becomes too academic or difficult to understand. I don't believe that gardening should ever become so complicated that it falls outside the ordinary person's reach. It has, after all, been practised for thousands of years by very ordinary people, and I don't see why it should now become the preserve of a handful of so-called experts. I have been gardening successfully for more than a decade, and all of my experience was gained from trial, error and the helpful guidance shared with me by those who had travelled the path longer than I had.

Gardeners, you will discover, are a funny breed. It is one of the few occupations where those who practice it are not only happy to share their knowledge, their time and their seeds and cuttings but also seem to delight in doing so. Perhaps it is because they recognise just how generous nature has been to them or perhaps it is just the simple and slow pace of life that nature dictates that makes them this way. I now try to share some of that wealth of information with you, confident in the knowledge that you too will pass it on somewhere down the line.

In this book, I will be sharing ways to expand your raised bed gardening to a different level. We will explore design in a little more depth as well as considering a far more comprehensive range of plants to grow. Whether your ambitions are just to augment your homegrown supplies or to dive right in and try to grow all of the vegetables you and your family consume, at the end of this book you will have all the knowledge you need to achieve your goals.

Hopefully, the first book in this series has already demonstrated just how productive this type of gardening can be and what a fantastic yield you can achieve in a relatively small space. Now we will consider ways to expand on that yield and also to bring in a whole range of more advanced crops that you might once have considered too difficult to grow yourself. You should have overcome that initial lack of confidence by now and be eager to build on that foundation that the first book laid for you.

Another aspect we will be looking at will be expanding your season so that you can reap the benefits of winter crops that are so often ignored by the small-scale gardener. These provide a vital harvest at a time when so many gardens lie idle or only support a cover crop. All of this new information I will endeavour to convey in the same simple terminology that I hope dominates this entire series. I want this to be a gradual and enjoyable learning experience rather than an attempt to over-complicate what should not be an overly complicated subject. Gardening, at the end of the day, should be a pleasure. One that helps sustain you and your family and the environment at the same time.

1

LAYOUTS

*a*t this stage, I am working on the assumption that the reader has read the Introduction to Raised Bed gardening or has had a season or two of gardening under his or her belt using the raised bed method. The fact that you have chosen to push on and expand your knowledge demonstrates that you have found that the method works and hopefully have become as enthusiast about raised beds as I am. It is a very practical method, and if it would only cause me to lose weight or stop losing hair, it would, in my opinion, be perfect.

Now it is time to move forward and turn your garden into something of a small farm. The temptation at this stage is to just cram in as many raised beds as possible and get growing, but I would urge a little patience here. Now that the whole concept is no longer new, you can start to consider not only the practicalities but also the design features that you most value. We have looked at some of the materials that beds can be made of in the last book. In this book, we are going to look at some more of these and also at some more daring designs. As always, good design starts on paper before it is put onto the ground.

The thing you must grasp is that you are not limited just to boxes and right rectangles. I always believe that even the most functional of gardens can include some design elements that will add to the aesthetic appeal. There is no reason why a raised bed garden should not be both pleasing to the eye and functional at the same time. When you first start with this method, it is new and, as with most things in life, it is best to keep things simple. Now is the time to be more daring and the best place to do that is on a piece of paper.

Firstly, you need to look at your existing beds and decide what worked and what didn't. Were your beds placed where there would catch that ideal six to eight hours a day of sunlight? Could you have made access more simple and was water readily available? If these crucial criteria were all met, then you will probably want to continue to garden where you do at the moment. If not, then now is the time to search for a more suitable environment. If the existing garden is perfectly placed, you will need to consider whether you simply want to add on to what you have already or start from scratch. It may seem like a waste of time pulling existing beds apart and rebuilding, but in reality, a few days of extra work will fade into oblivion once you have created the garden of your dreams. Be daring and dream big is my advice. You will also have learned a great deal about the materials you built with the first time around, and you might believe that it is time for a change.

What I want you to grasp is that beds can be of any shape that you care to build them. You need to consider ease of access from all sides, but you know that already, so are well placed on incorporating that into your new design. I have known gardeners to become so enthralled with the raised bed concept that they converted their whole garden to this format. All beds were raised but by the innovative use of both height and shape, and they were able to produce something breathtakingly beautiful both for their vegetable garden and for their flower garden.

Once you have decided beyond doubt where the raised bed garden is to be, you will need to measure it out and draw it to scale. In the first book, where simple shapes were used, you were able to do a reasonably rough measurement. Now you will need to be more accurate and you will probably need to use a long tape measure and some fixed points to be sure that what you have on paper corresponds to what you will have on the ground. We will deal with this part of the design process in much more depth in the book on Urban Gardening, which is part of this series.

In order to measure accurately, you are going to use a system called triangulation. This requires you to measure from two set points to create a triangle, thus ensuring that the point you are measuring to remains fixed. For example, if a point is five meters from a fence, it is very difficult when putting it on paper, to know where on the drawing it should go. If on the other hand, that same point is ten meters from one end of the fence and nine meters from the other end of the fence, that position becomes fixed. This means that as long as you have taken your measurements correctly, the position you have marked can only be in the position where the nine and ten-meter marks intersect.

It will take a while to get the plan laid out on paper but take your time over this part of the operation because it is crucial. It is the accuracy you produce now that enables you to reproduce your design from paperback onto the ground at a later stage. I would recommend that you draw out the garden on graph paper after deciding what scale fits the paper most appropriately. At the end of the measuring out process, you should have an accurate and to scale plan of the outline of the garden, including any features like sheds or trees. You should also have an accurate mark as to where taps and water sources are and where north is. Once you are sure that the plan is a to-scale representation of what is on the ground then make several photocopies. Pour a large cup of tea (red wine will do as a substitute) and let your imagination go wild.

Certain practicalities will always remain important. Your paths will need to be wide enough to accommodate a wheelbarrow comfortably, you will need to be able to access the plants easily without having to walk on the beds, and you will need to consider where the sun will fall. Other than that, you can be as creative as you want to be. I have seen star-shaped beds, U shaped beds and round beds. Even a spiral can be made using packed rocks. This gives you a spiral that gradually mounts at the centre in a shape reminiscent of a snail's shell and makes for a beautiful eye-catching focal point.

Always be on the lookout for inspiration, and you will be surprised where you find it. Landscape architects designed many of those desiccated looking beds you see in shopping centre car parks. Beneath the sad looking plants there is often a creative structural plan, and there may be ideas there that help you develop the skeleton for your garden. Garden magazines and the internet are teeming with design ideas, and by now you are probably already addicted to some of the many gardening shows on television. What you will need to do is sit down with the photocopied plans of the garden skeleton and draw out different options until you come up with a design that pleases you. Don't expect this to be a one attempt and all is done process. It requires numerous re-workings and even the most experienced of garden designers draws and redraws before he gets a result that he is ultimately happy with. That is why I suggested taking several photocopies of the plan you measured. You can sketch away to your heart's content and then start a new plan if you don't achieve a pleasing enough result.

The drawing may be two dimensional, but that doesn't mean the garden needs to be. Think about beds of differing heights as well as arbours between beds or trellises up which climbers and vines can scramble. If you have the room, then throw in a water feature or a couple of nice outdoor sculptures. It doesn't matter if you don't have any and can't afford them. If they are built into the plan now, they can be added at a later stage once you have worn your spouse down with constant hints and suggestions as to what you would like if you had a little spare cash.

At the end of any design process, my kitchen floor is covered with balls of paper that bare testimony to early failed drawings. Hopefully, however, somewhere on the table is a pristine design that perfectly adheres to both my desires and the practicalities of the garden I want. Each of those failures on the floor added a little something to what turned out to be the end result. For many of my gardening acquaintances and me, the design process is one of the more creative parts of gardening so wallow in it rather than shy from it.

In my use of the pen and paper approach, I am something of a dinosaur. Today there is a myriad of garden design computer programs that eliminate the need for piles of paper and go a little way toward saving the planet at the same time. Unfortunately, as far as my abilities are concerned, the planet will have to suffer a little longer because I simply lack the computer design skills. Those that have patiently tried to train me in that direction have all eventually had to accept that I have the computer abilities of a somewhat dim-witted King Charles spaniel.

Whatever route you choose to follow in the design process, always have practicality in the back of your mind. Some materials lend themselves freely to curves and bends while others don't. I like to decide well in advance what material the beds will be made of and then design accordingly, rather than the other way around. Knowing what materials you will be using often determines what bed shapes can be built. If I am working with wooden beds, for example, it is not possible to make one in the form of a circle. We looked at several materials in the first book on raised beds, but you might want to skip ahead to the next chapter to look at some slightly different options before you make a final decision.

It is also wise to know beforehand what your paths are to be made from. If you are just throwing down bark or wood chips, then it won't be a problem, but if you want a more rigid material such as brushed concrete, then you must consider when during the build process this will be poured. Be realistic about your ability to build the garden you design if you are planning on doing the work yourself. There are few things more frustrating than having the perfect design on paper but then finding you lack the ability to convert those plans to reality. You can, of course, hire the services of a professional but please speak to them in advance so that they can have some input as to what is practically possible and what can only be done with the backup of a team from NASA.

I am hoping that all that you have read in this book so far points clearly to one thing. Thinking things out in advance is critical. The more complex your design, the more difficult the build and the more accurate you will need to be when laying the plan out on the ground. You will need to find that elusive balance between great design and functionality. On the one hand, I am trying to encourage you to be daring, and on the other, I probably seem like I am holding you back by reminding you of the restrictions imposed by practicality. Somewhere between those two parameters, there is a solution and if you take your time, seek outside inspiration and are creative, you will find it. I find it helps to remind myself that I am working with natural materials and that by combining those with a well thought out design, I can't go too far wrong. Most of the ugly things we see in this world do not incorporate natural materials very much.

So far, we have been looking at this whole design process from the point of view of fixed beds. There is the option, however, of making beds that are movable and with raised beds, this is entirely feasible. There are a few reasons for a gardener to choose to go down this route. The most common is where only a small area is available, and it becomes necessary to move the beds during the day to access the maximum amount of light. This is often the case on apartment patios. As the light moves, part of the patio may become shaded by the building or neighbouring buildings. By only moving the beds from one side of the patio to the other, this lack of light issue might be overcome. Another instance might be where there is only a little amount of space on a terrace or deck. The raised beds can be placed and planted but should the space be needed as an entertainment area occasionally; the beds could be temporarily moved out of the way.

There is any number of easy ways to make mobile beds. They can be made from plastic milk crates with some lining to retain the soil, or they can be purpose-built. Something of a similar shape to a table but with raised sides to hold soil and some drainage holes would make a fine bed to grow a few herbs or some of the smaller vegetables such as carrots and radishes. If it were to have wheels, then moving it from one place to another would become that much easier.

We looked quite extensively at building raised beds in the first book on the subject. In the next chapter, we will look at some slightly less common options.

2

UNORTHODOX RAISED BED MATERIALS

Once you have drawn out your plan, you now need to reproduce that drawing on the ground. This requires you to reverse the process with as much accuracy as possible. You will need to take out your extra-long tape measure again and using the same fixed points as you did for the plan you will now need to mark your beds out on the ground upon which the garden is to be built. You can lay them out using pegs and sticks, but I suggest you pop into your local builders' merchant and purchase a can of marking out spray. Laying out the bed with strings and canes almost always leads to problems as they move so easily.

With the corners of each bed marked out from the drawing, it is a relatively simple matter to join up the dots using the spray and a straight edge if you don't think you can manage free hand.

Once your beds are drawn out on the ground, you will start to get a far better feel for what the finished garden is going to look like. If possible, try to get a bit of a birds-eye view by looking down on the beds from a first-floor window or even a step ladder. This will be your final opportunity to make sure that what you have marked out corresponds precisely with your scale plan.

Wooden frames have traditionally dominated raised beds. There are many different options and here are some that we have not looked at in as much depth as we did the wooden beds in book one. Each comes with advantages and disadvantages which you will need to consider in terms of your particular circumstances, building capabilities and budget.

Cement blocks are sturdy, long-lasting and allow you the opportunity to make beds of almost any shape. Laying blocks is quite physically demanding, but if you can handle the physical exercise, they are not that difficult to lay. You will need to run a small concrete foundation and then lay the blocks using sand and cement. This may seem a little bit like the work of an expert bricklayer, but it is relatively easy though the blocks are heavy. As long as you can mix a four to one sharp sand to cement mix and use a spirit level, then laying blocks is not beyond the reach of any home handyman. Another factor that might help you be a little more confident is that you are unlikely to need to go more than two courses high. If you were to set about making a building with no experience, then I might be a little less quick to encourage you to give it a go yourself.

Blocks come in differing widths and you want the wider ones which are six inches wide. They are heavier but they will give you excellent beds that will last for many years. For a more superior appearance, you can plaster the outsides with a water-proof plaster and finish off the tops with wood or tiles. I come from an area rich in limestone, and once I have built my beds, I clad them in flat pieces of stone which makes the beds look like they are made from stone but at a fraction of the price. To attach the stone to the blocks, you mix some lime powder with sand and cement, and they stick quite easily.

A totally different effect can be had by building beds from straw bales. This is one of the easiest materials to use as you just lay the bales end to end and you have a deep bed in which to lay your planting medium. They are cheap, usually quite readily available and the whole garden can be built in virtually no time. If you want to put up plant supports or trellis, the posts can just be stabbed into the bales themselves. There is nothing new about this system, and it has been used for hundreds of years in various places throughout the world.

It is essential to understand the difference between straw and hay. Straw is made from the leftover stems of crops such as wheat, barley or alfalfa. Hay is made from dried cut grass. Hay will break down much more quickly than straw, but more importantly, it has not had the heads cut off before being baled, and so contains seeds. Not only will there be grass seeds but it will also contain the seeds of any weeds that will have grown in the grass. I am not saying don't use hay; you need to be aware that it does not come with the same benefits of straw, and you will have a weed problem.

Beds built from straw bales will generally last only one season if you live in a hot and wet area, two at the most. As the straw breaks down, it adds other nutrients to your beds which is a plus. When you are done with the bales, it makes a good winter mulch or can be mixed with manure to rot down into great compost slowly. New beds can then be built using the same method. Straw is porous meaning that beds will drain quite quickly though I find the bales tend to absorb excess water which helps keeps the whole bed moist.

If you feel that this is a good route for you then make sure that you layout your beds on a dry day. Moving wet straw bales is a lot more physically demanding than moving dry ones. Another advantage that straw bales have is that you get to change your garden design every year or two. When the time comes to exchange the old bales for new ones you might like to shake things up a bit and go for a whole garden makeover which few other raised bed materials offer.

Galvanised metal is one of my favourite choices when building raised beds. At first, the idea sounds more practical than attractive, but I frame the individual sheets with pieces of two by four timber. This makes them easy to bolt together while at the same time making the beds far more attractive and less utilitarian looking than if I were to simply hold the sheets up with stakes. It makes them more secure, and a dark stain on the wooden frames contrasts nicely with the clean look of the metal. It is easy enough to cut the sheets with an angle grinder so I can get a variety of bed shapes, but I cannot make curved forms using this material. Some companies supply pre-made galvanised beds which just need to be bolted together. These come with preformed rounded ends which is quite pleasing to the eye. They also offer a choice of coloured powder coat finishes so you aren't restricted to just that shiny galvanised effect.

If you live in an agricultural area, you can sometimes purchase galvanised feed troughs from agricultural suppliers. These tend to be round with a four-foot diameter and three feet high. If you want round beds, then this may be an easy route to go down. Just have some feed troughs delivered, drill plenty of drainage holes in the bottom and fill with growing medium, and you are good to go.

Galvanised beds come with many advantages, but there are some drawbacks you might need to consider. They do get hotter than wooden beds and you may need to water slightly more often. They also don't drain so you will need to ensure that the ground beneath these beds is free draining or your beds will become a swamp. That said, I still believe that they provide a very practical, long-lasting and attractive option.

Some people have taken to building the walls of their beds from old car tires, and this has caused something of a controversy in the gardening world. Tires are free, readily available and easy to build with. They can also be laid in a wide array of shapes. The controversy arises over the fact that they are made from petroleum-based materials. Whilst nobody has done tests as to whether or not these will leach into the soil and cause toxicity, the possibility does exist.

What I believe is that even if the tires do break down, they are not going to do so in a hurry. It should, therefore, be relatively safe if you only use them for a year or two and then replace them. I should also point out that I have absolutely no scientific evidence for this theory and that you should therefore not regard it as of any value what so ever. I have, however, been growing potatoes in tires for years and so far have suffered no noticeable ill effects other than a slight thickening of the waist. This could equally be attributed to red wine consumption which does take place from time to time.

There is one other option for raised beds that is not so much a material option as a change in methodology. This method, known as the hotbed method, has been used since Victorian times to grow plants during the colder months. The bottom three-quarters of the bed is filled with manure while the top quarter is then filled with your choice of growing medium. As the manure breaks down, it rapidly increases the temperature of the soil, and this gives you a longer growing season and enables you to grow plants such as pineapples which you would not usually be able to grow unless you lived closer to the equator.

Victorian gardeners were famed for the ability to put unusual food on the tables of their wealthy employers at times when things like pineapple would only have been an expensive imported luxury. The hotbed was one of their favourite methods for doing this, and most Victorian glasshouses had a raised bed built into them. The beds tended to be built from brick and were usually about two feet high. If you want to experiment with this system, you could do so as long as your raised bed were at least eighteen inches high. It works both indoors and outdoors but the extra heat lasts only for about two months at which point the beds need to be emptied and refilled.

Whatever material you decide on, remember that the plants don't care, what your raised bed is doing as acting as a container for an ideal growing medium. The choice you make, therefore depends on your budget, your building ability and what sort of look you want to achieve. If you start by looking through reclaimed material yards and things like Craigslist and the internet, you may well find bargains that influence your choice of material.

One of the most impressive raised bed gardens that I have seen was made from a series of old bathtubs laid end to end down a hill. Watering was done by filling the top bath bed which was connected to the next one via a pipe from the plug hole to the overflow hole. Gradually by just adding water to the top bed, it would flow down to the lowest bed, and the depth of the baths was perfect for raised beds. I am not suggesting that you rush out and buy up every old bath you can get your hands on. I am only offering this as an example of what a little out of the box thinking can produce, and to show just what a versatile system the raised bed garden can provide.

3

EXPERIMENTING WITH VARIOUS PLANT GROWING TECHNOLOGIES

*O*ne of the things that many gardeners struggle to come to terms with is that gardening is as much art as it is science. Because we live in a world where so much is human-made and is defined by rigidly fixed criteria, it is easy to assume that a fixed set of rules governs everything we deal with. In gardening, this is very often not the case. Here we are dealing with nature, and many of her rules are more flexible and forgiving than those we choose to impose upon ourselves. It follows, therefore, that there is more than one method of gardening in just about every instance you can think of. Personally, I like the fact that I'm not restricted to just one tightly governed way of doing things. It gives me the freedom to experiment, try different methods and be that little bit more creative than I might have been in another field of work. This is not to suggest that we can simply do what we want to and go against all of the rules that nature does apply, but at the same time, she allows us a level of freedom that we may not be used to.

For some people, this lack of rigidity can be a little disconcerting. Rules offer some people clarity and the security of knowing that they are not going wrong. In this chapter, we are going to be looking at some alternative ways of doing things. They are neither right nor wrong. They merely offer the gardener an alternative approach and very often, as the gardener grows in experience and confidence, he tends to reach a point where he can mix and match different techniques to create something that becomes uniquely his own. Think of it as being like a recipe. The first time you make a new dish you diligently follow the rules, accurately measure out quantities and stick to a strict palette of ingredients. Once you've cooked the dish a couple of times, you quickly reach a point where you can place your mark on it to make it more unique to yourself.

I believe that gardeners and chefs have a great deal in common. The world of cooking would not be the same, and our diets would be a whole lot blander if chefs didn't step out of their comfort zone and push the boundaries. In my opinion, the same thing applies to gardening. It is a field in which each of us has learnt and benefited from the experiments and experience of those who went before us. I wouldn't go so far as to say that I believe it is beholden on us to explore new methods. I do think, though, that experimentation can benefit the whole gardening community. Even if you are one of those people who is happier when governed by rules, I would still encourage you to have a look at these techniques and see if there is not something to be gained from incorporating some of the ideas into your own garden. As ancient as it is, gardening remains a continually evolving process, and mixing and matching is one way in which you can develop your skills as a gardener. As well as stamping your unique way of doing things onto your gardening, you will be pioneering new methods for the gardeners that come after you. The methods that we're about to look at are actually quite old and have been well tested; it is only by adding your own subtle twists to them that you may see something new emerge. I should point out that my theory on experimentation in the garden is not popular with everyone and many gardeners believe that we should stick diligently to the rules. I will leave it to you to decide just how much or how little you want to combine the different techniques. Personally, I am as attracted to the art as I am to the science. With all of my experimenting over the years, I have had my share of failures, but I have always tried to learn from them. The adventures they have provided have helped to keep my passion for gardening as alive today as it was when I first started out.

The first alternative system we're going to look at is straw bale gardening. I know that we have already looked at this material in the context of using the bales as the actual frame of our raised beds. In this instance, we are going to look at them as a means of replacing the planting medium with the straw bales them-selves. In other words, we are not going to use them to create our frame; we are going to use them actually to grow our plants. There are several reasons for going down this route. Straw bales can be used as a planting medium on top of any base, including concrete, and they use less labour as there is not any digging or tilling involved. Because they are warmer, they can dramatically extend the growing season both in the spring and in the autumn. They are particularly useful, however, in situations where getting soil or other planting mediums is difficult either because of price, availability or access. Easy to move around, they are cheap and generally tend to be readily available.

Growing on bales offers immediate height, so your physical effort is reduced, they can be used in small spaces, and they require virtually no weeding. Any weeding that is required tends to be very easy because the roots of the weeds are not bound securely into the straw. With this method, you also eliminate the risk of soil-borne diseases. Because they can be used on any type of base, this method is ideal when gardening on concrete surfaces and therefore provides a method for people living in an apartment to grow plants on their terrace. Finally, their rough surface means you will hardly ever have problems from either snails or slugs.

Of course, as with any other type of gardening, this system does come without some drawbacks. Straw bales dry up more quickly, and water control becomes very important. You will also need to fertilise them with some sort of organic fertiliser because this is what will supply the food for your plants, especially in the initial stages.

You can typically purchase straw bales from garden centres, stables or home depots. The best place to get them, however, is directly from the farmer and the best straw is always going to be that made with organic material. They can be made from wheat, oats, rye or barley. You can also use linseed or flax if it is available, both of which are slower to break down because of their oil content. There will be occasions when you are unable to get straw bales, and all that you have access to is hay. The difference between hay and straw is that the flowering heads are incorporated into the hay bales. This is quite a crucial point because it means that weeds will become an issue. That said, if you don't mind doing a bit of weeding, the nutrient supply in hay bales is actually far higher than it is in straw bales.

Before you can use straw bales as a growing medium, they first need to be prepared. There are a couple of ways of doing this, but they both amount to the same thing. The objective is to get the bales to a point where they are starting to decompose because it is the decomposing plant material that will provide the food for your new plants. Both methods of doing this will take about two weeks.

Once you have purchased your straw bales, place them in the position where you intend to do your gardening before you start conditioning them. Dry bales are easy to move around, but wet ones become considerably heavier. If you have built raised beds and are using the bales as your growing medium, simply drop your bales into the beds. The next thing you must do is wet the bales down. On the first day, water them thoroughly and then on days two and three water them again on a daily basis. After that, on days four to ten water and feed them with a liquid feed such as compost tea or manure soaked in water until it has dissolved. If you don't fancy making your liquid fertiliser, there are commercial products that you can buy, but you will need to find an organic option.

From the eleventh day to the thirteenth day, you can stop the feeding and just keep the bales damp which will now require less water as they will have started to become saturated. Finally, on the fourteenth day, plunge your hand into the bale to test the heat. The interior should be warm but still slightly cooler than body temperature. This heating process has been brought about by the breaking down of the plant material in a fermentation like process. At its peak, which should have occurred at around day six or seven, the interior of a bale could climb to as high as 65° c (150°F). At that temperature, it would have been far too hot for plants to survive but now as it cools it is in a perfect state for plant growth.

The second method is slightly different, but you are trying to achieve precisely the same result and you should opt for which- ever method suits you. On days one, three and five, sprinkle the bales with a generous quantity of dry organic fertiliser and then water in generously. On days two four and six simply soak the bales without adding any feed. On days seven eight and nine, you feed again with one and a half cups of fertiliser per pale per day.

From day eleven, you start watering daily again and by day fourteen, the temperature within the bales should be just below body temperature. As you can see, this is a different route to get to the same place and your method will often be dictated by the choice of fertilisers you have available. It usually takes about two gallons to soak a bale but rather than getting into a complicated water measuring situation, simply apply enough water that it starts to run out the bottom of the bale. As the inside of the bale starts to break down, don't be surprised if you start to see a few mushrooms appearing on the surface. In fact, this is a good sign as it proves that the bacterial action is well underway.

As we have already mentioned, there are no hard and fast rules here. Once you become accustomed to working with the bales, you will start to develop the experience to alter the recipe to suit your personal tastes and conditions.

Finally, after two weeks of conditioning, your bales are at last ready, and you can now plant directly into them. If you are planting seeds, then sprinkle a layer of soilless seed compost so that they have something to get rooted into initially. If you are planting seedlings, then make a hole big enough to accommo-date the whole root ball then pop the plant out of its container and plant the whole root ball into the straw. You will follow the same planting distances as you would if you were planting into a soil-based medium.

You can grow just about any plant that you would be able to grow under normal circumstances but be aware that the roots will not gain quite as much support as they would in denser soil. This means that top-heavy plants like corn will need to be staked. Placing stakes and other supports is dead easy because you can just stab them down into the bale. Most of the larger plants that might be prone to tipping can be overcome in smaller dwarf varieties, so this might also be something to consider.

Root crops like carrots and turnips will gradually weaken the bale. This won't be an issue if your bales are contained in a raised bed, but if they are standing in the open it will shorten their longevity. As I seldom get more than one season from my bales, this does not really alter my planting plan. Potatoes do fine in bales if they are planted at a depth of about six inches. They can be earthed up by just continuing to cover with straw rather than soil. Leave an inch or two of leaf protruding each time. If you want to avoid the earthing up process then just plant them deeper. Sixteen to eighteen inches should give you a generous crop.

Whether you are growing from seed or from seedlings, you will need to water in with a fine sprinkler and then water at least once daily. Poke your finger into the bales near your plants from time to time to ensure that the growing medium is always slightly damp. With bales, drying out can occur relatively quickly, and one of the downsides to this method is that you will need to be more attentive than you might need to be in a soil-based medium.

Once a week you will need to feed your plants with a liquid feed. There are dozens of options. You may have been making your own fertiliser tea, but you could also use products such a blood meal, fish meal or a seaweed-based product. All of these are available at garden centres.

At the end of the growing season, you can examine your bales and decide if they are in good enough condition to use for one more season. In my experience, they seldom are, especially if I have produced a lot of root crops that year. If you are lucky, store the bales somewhere dry until the following spring and then reuse them. If not, mix them into your compost to break down or use them as a mulch on other beds.

SQUARE FOOT GARDENING:

Square foot gardening is a concept that has been around since the nineteen-eighties. It was the brainchild of a retired engineer by the name of Mel Bartholomew, and his boof Square Foot Gardening has gone on to become a gardening classic. Once Mel retired, he devoted himself to gardening and with an engineer's practical approach to things he was soon finding ways to reduce labour and increase yields. The method he invented is said to enable a gardener to produce the same quantity of crops in twenty per cent of the space.

In America, the concept gained huge momentum and Mel soon become something of a celebrity with a very popular television series that ran for several years. The method is particularly pertinent to people who want to produce vegetables on a small amount of space. As the name implies, beds are divided up into one-foot squares and then each square is planted with a different crop or companion plant. What makes their productivity so high is that no land is lost to paths and the squares are heavily planted so that weeding is kept to a minimum.

If you follow Mel's suggestion, then beds will be four foot by four foot thus providing sixteen planting squares. This easily facilitates access from all sides without the need to walk on the bed. If this sounds familiar, it is because the same thinking went into the raised bed system, and the two methods offer plenty of scope to overlap one another. If you have existing raised beds, you can simply divide them up into one-foot squares. To do this, you can nail a latticework of wooden laths to form a trellis of one-foot squares over the bed, or you can mark out the squares with string. Entirely how you do this will depend on the material your raised beds are made of and how rigidly you want to stick to the system.

If you don't have a raised bed already, you can make one out of six to twelve-inch wide planks with lap joints cut out of them every twelve inches. The planks then simply slot into one another, giving you sixteen-foot square beds. At the end of the season, the planks are then just detached and stored for the next season. If you are planning on gardening with children, you might want to drop the bed size down to three foot by three foot. You will only have nine beds, but the children should be able to reach most parts of the bed without needing to walk on the soil or the plants.

Using this method, there is hardly any thinning required and you, therefore, use far less seed. Each square is planted with a predetermined number of plants depending on the crop. See the chart below. Rather than sprinkling a whole row of seed and then thinning, you drop just two or three seeds into the requisite number of planting holes and then just snip off the two weakest seedlings with a scissor once they set their first true leaves.

As with other raised bed systems, it usually is easy to attach a trellis or other support for climbing crops. As we have already seen, theses taller plants will need to be planted on the northern end of the bed in the northern hemisphere and the southern end in the southern hemisphere so that they don't cast a shadow over your smaller crops.

Another secret to the square foot gardening method was, of course, the growing mix. Mel's recipe calls for one third peat moss, one-third vermiculite and one-third compost or potting soil. The recipe is still widely used by raised bed gardeners and you will often hear the term Mel's mix or Mel's magic mix in gardening circles. Now at least you will know what people are referring to.

If you are like me and you question the environmental impact of using peat moss, then it can be replaced by coir, potting soil or rice husks. Vermiculite is a mineral that is mined for different purposes, but in gardening terms, it is used for its moisture retention.

Though you will often hear the term Mel's mix, it is far from the only growing medium available to the ardent raised bed gardener, and we will be looking at this subject in more detail further into the book.

Plant	Plants per Square	Plant	Plants per Square
Arugula	4	Okra	1
Basil	4	Onion	4
Bean-Bush	1-4	Parsnips	16
Bean-Pole	1-4	Peas	1
Beets	9	Peppers	1
Brussels Sprouts	1	Pigeon Peas	1
Cabbage	1	Pumpkin	1
Chinese Cabbage	9	Radicchio	2-4
Carrots	16	Radish	16
Corn	4	Rhubarb	1
Cucumber	2	Rutabaga	4
Eggplant	1	Shallots	4
Greens-baby harvest	16	Spinach	9
Greens-mature harvest	4-8	Squash-summer	1
Kale	1	Squash-winter	1
Kohlrabi	4	Sweet Potato	1
Leeks	4-8	Swiss Chard	4
Lettuce-heading	1-4	Tomatillo	1
Lettuce-loose leaf	4	Tomatoes	1
		Turnips	9
Broccoli	1 (18" spacing is best)		
Cauliflower	1 (18" spacing is best)		

Herbs	Herbs per Square	Fruit	Fruit per Square
Basil	4	Garden Huckleberry	1
Calendula	1-4	Melon	1 (18"-24" spacing is best)
Chives	9	Watermelon	1 (18"-24" spacing is best)
Cilantro	9		
Dill	1		
Fennel	4		
Oregano	1		
Parsley	1		
Rosemary	1		
Sage	1		
Tarragon	1		
Thyme	4		

THE NO-DIG METHOD:

This is another gardening method that has quite a long pedigree. It works on the concept that the less you manipulate the soil, the more the microbes and organisms will increase, and the healthier your soil will become. Digging is hard physical work, and although the raised bed method reduces the amount of digging to be done and cuts out much of the bending, many gardeners are happy to avoid it altogether.

No-dig gardening was not devised with the raised bed gardener in mind, but as a way to reduce work when gardening in open ground. Fortunately, this method combines very well with raised bed methodology and you, therefore, have the opportunity to explore the best of both worlds. We will start looking at how it is done in the open ground and then have a look at how to combine the methodology with our raised beds.

The idea is that a garden can be created, even on grass or weeds, without needing to pre-dig the soil. The area to be planted should be covered in a deep layer of compost, and over time, lack of light and air will kill the underlying plants. Often when creating the first bed, the gardener will lay down sheets of cardboard to make it doubly difficult for weeds and grass to survive. The compost will be laid on top of that to a depth of about six inches. A month later, the bed can be planted. Some weeds will make it through the compost, but they will do so in a very weakened state and are therefore extremely easy to deal with.

Once the crop is harvested, simply add another two to three inches of compost, firm down lightly, and the bed is ready to be planted again.

When using this method on the ground, there will be places where really aggressive weeds demand firmer action, and in cases like this, a sheet of dark plastic can be laid over the planned bed for a month. After that, the plastic can be rolled back, and a two to three-inch layer of compost spread before replacing the plastic sheet over the bed, complete with its layer of compost. After another month, the bed will be ready for planting. Without even removing the plastic, holes can be simply cut through where the new plants are wanted, and the seedlings can be planted into the layer of compost through the hole.

On some studies done side by side with the traditional dig system, yields are in the region of twenty-five per cent higher with far less physical effort having been brought into play. Furthermore, analysis of the soil has revealed that it remains more tightly bound together which gives it a better structure.

If you have been gardening in raised beds for a while, you will know that much of what you have just read is very similar to the techniques you will already be used to using. Before filling your beds, you may already have been putting down a layer of cardboard to suppress weeds and most of the digging you have been doing has been merely to incorporate new compost or growing medium at the end of each season.

To combine the two methods, the only real difference would be that after harvesting your crops, you would now just top up the bed with two or three inches of healthy compost. Other than firming it down by giving it a few slaps with the back of a shovel, there would be no further preparation to do. Don't worry if the new layer of compost is slightly deeper than the tops of your beds. Compost is continuously breaking down, and it will soon reduce in depth. It is important to firmly tamp it down because plants will not grow as successfully if the compost is too loose.

Deep digging and double digging are methods that gardeners have been using for centuries, but science is now having its say. What it is telling us is that much of that back-breaking labour could have been avoided. When gardening in open ground on heavy clay soils, there would have been benefits from intense digging. I think that this is where this system somehow became accepted practice. It is still widely taught today at many horticultural and gardening colleges and universities, but it now looks as though the no-dig method will begin to fall from favour.

VERTICAL GARDENING:

Vertical gardening is a method of growing plants in containers suspended from walls. It uses very similar methods to those use in raised beds, and the two systems can be incorporated and will complement each other perfectly.

What vertical gardening does, is that it utilises space that would otherwise have been lost to the gardener. It is very useful if you have a walled garden or even just a bare wall that would provide you somewhere to hang your containers. It is an excellent method for gaining extra capacity where space is at a premium and the apartment patio is the perfect example.

What the wall does is provide support for whatever hanging garden system you opt for. You increase your growing area and at the same time, you turn what might have been a bland or even ugly wall into something of abundant beauty. This system really can provide the gardener with some stunning results and can be used for edible crops or ornamental ones or perhaps a combination of the two.

There are many ways of turning walls into growing space, but whichever method you decide to go for, you must ensure that there is no possibility of water ingress. The method is becoming quite popular, and as a result, there are now companies that specialise in kits for this type kind of gardening. If that is out of your budget or you simply prefer to create your own vertical beds, there are other options. These include suspended containers made from horticultural fabric with pocket like planting spaces sown in, wooden or plastic planters on hooks or even plastic bottles suspended in frames. That might sound a little ugly, but as soon as it is planted up, the foliage transforms the wall into something almost exotic looking.

As with all container gardening, watering is something that needs to be taken into consideration, and you will need to feed your plants from time to time with an organic liquid feed. There will be more on this subject in the book on container gardening later in this series. Generally, these walls tend to be small enough that they can be watered just with a watering can or a wand attached to a hose. If you are planning on really going for it and covering a lot of wall space, you might want to consider building a drip irrigation system into your construction plan. Some of the premanufactured systems come with an inbuilt method of redirecting excess water from the planters down to the lower ones so that by just watering at the top, water finds its way through the system right down the bottom.

This system is becoming so prevalent that it is being incorporated into whole apartment blocks, internal and external walls of hotels and offices and home developments. As an unexpected side benefit, it has now been discovered that having a wall of green material provides a building with excellent insulation against both heat and sound. Another surprise benefit is that it dramatically cuts down graffiti because the graffiti 'artists' are no longer tempted by the blank canvas a bare wall offered.

4

A LOOK AT SOME ADVANCED CROPS
FOR RAISED BEDS

*I*n the first book in this series, we looked at growing some of the plants that are most commonly consumed by the home gardener. In this chapter, we are going to kick this up a notch and instead focus on some of the plants you may not typically have considered or had thought might be too difficult. These plants may not be something you would ordinarily consume on a daily basis but would perhaps have purchased from time to time, either when the price was right or to add some variety to your diet. With your growing medium so easy to control, I am hoping that plants that were once thought of as something to eat every now and then, might now be grown more widely.

CELERY:

Let's face facts; celery can be a temperamental plant even in the best of scenarios. As you will see, the raised bed option will help overcome many common problems when growing this plant, but you need to balance that out against the fact that global warming is making things harder. Big commercial growers tend to produce this crop in tunnels that often incorporate air temperature control. Although that means they can control the climate, they are not able to produce plants that are as tasty as real homegrown celery.

The list of problems that celery poses to the home grower can seem somewhat overwhelming. They include bolting (at the drop of a hat), black heart, brittle or bitter leaves, too many leaves or they can just be too tough. With a pedigree like that, one solution is to say fine; I'll just buy a bunch next time I'm down the supermarket.

I want to urge you to be a little more adventurous here. Firstly, you will grow as a gardener even if you fail; secondly, you will eventually overcome the most common problems. Finally, and this is most important, once you master this plant, you will be able to casually give some to other gardeners who will probably have gone down this path and given up. I'm not suggesting that you boast here, but you should know that opportunity exists.

Celery is fussy about temperature and even when you have perfect raised beds, this is one little fly that nature is still able to drop into your ointment. If temperatures bounce up and down too much, celery panics and bolts. Bolting occurs when a plant says to itself "I'm going to die. I must produce offspring quickly." It then produces flowers and focuses all its attention on setting seed rather than on producing luscious green leaves.

If there is a risk of night temperatures dropping below 4.5° Celsius (40°F) then celery will be tempted to bolt. If you have grown your plants from seed indoors, or bought in seedlings, hold them back until you are sure that the night time temperature will not fall below this. Because you are using a raised bed, it should be easy enough to put in a tunnel over part of the bed using hoops, and it will be simpler to keep temperatures more stable. This will also mean that there is some shade during the hottest time of the day and you, therefore, reduce that effect where temperatures bounce up and down which celery hates.

If your plant does show signs of bolting, then cut off the early flowers and this may encourage it to focus more energy on the leaves. Also, harvest some leaves from the plant which should then encourage it to produce more foliage. Even if your plant does bolt and gets away from you, all is not lost. The leaves can still be used in soups, or the plants can be left to do their own thing. They will get tall and covered in flowers which will be a boon for the local bees and butterflies. When fellow gardeners visit, you can tell them you have grown these plants to help the environment.

Another dreaded problem that makes many gardeners shudder is called black heart. The inner leaves die, and those that remain are tough. This is usually an indication of a lack of calcium in the soil and is one problem that carefully managed raised beds shouldn't present. Because the raised bed gardener is so diligent about adding well-rotted compost his soil is generally not prone to this problem. Topdressing with more compost helps ensure this never becomes an issue and regulates soil temperature. Some varieties have been bred to resist this problem. You might try 'Verde Pascal' or 'Conquistador'.

If the leaves are cracked, brittle, or are simply too tough, there are two probable reasons. There is a Boron deficiency, or the soil is getting too hot. Boron deficiency is unlikely as you have managed the soil so thoroughly, but just in case, add plenty of fertilizer tea. A more likely culprit is that the soil is becoming too hot. Ideally, you want to time your planting so that you can harvest in the autumn and avoid the hottest of the summer. Also, six hours of sun is enough for this plant so place them where they will get some shade from taller plants such as tomatoes or use that tunnel covered in shade cloth.

If you are growing your plants from seed, you will need to start them indoors or in the greenhouse ten weeks before you intend to plant them out. That is a long time to be nurturing seedlings, so time this so that they go out as the hottest months draw to a close. If it is too hot, hold them back until conditions are not so harsh. You will be best placed to be able to assess local conditions, but as all gardeners are learning, those predictions are becoming harder to make. This is a plant where the choice of variety can be really crucial. Speak to your local nurseryman or members of your garden club to see what varieties have worked well in the past.

EGGPLANT:

This is a great plant to grow, especially if you are a cook. An adventurous chef can do wonders with this plant, and they are often quite expensive at local supermarkets or greengrocers so it is definitely one to try. If you have become addicted to growing heirloom seeds, there are numerous varieties of both shape and colour that you simply won't see in most commercial outlets. All eggplants make handsome additions to the garden as well as providing a delicious crop. They are cousins of the tomato, the pepper and the potato (as well as deadly nightshade but let's not go there).

Start seeds indoors and plant out as seedlings only once you are sure that the last of the frosts have passed. As with most seedlings, they should be hardened off gradually before being planted into their final position. They need full sun and will take sixty to ninety days to reach harvest stage depending on local conditions. Ideally, they need a day time temperature of 26° Celsius (80°F), but night-time temperatures shouldn't go too much below 18°c (65°F).

Stake them when you plant them and feed them every two weeks with an organic liquid feed. If you want enormous fruits, then leave only two or three per plant. If you are happy with slightly smaller fruit, then you will get more per plant if you let them all grow. Pick them when they are ready to eat. They don't store well but you get a little extra shelf life if you clip them off with an inch or so of stem still attached. If you are planning on saving the seed, then you will need to keep one of the fruits until it has gone past the edible stage and had started to dry out. Grate the base of the fruit over a bowl of water using a vegetable grater. The seed will sink and can then be dried for use the following season.

The reason this fruit can be difficult to grow is that they are susceptible to pests who love them as much as gardeners do. As we are organic gardeners, we are not able to defend ourselves as easily as those who are happy to just blast pests with toxic chemicals. That does not mean, however, that we are defenceless.

The most prevalent pest on these plants is the Colorado beetle. He is easy to identify little critter with a golden shell and ten pronounced black stripes. If you are observing your plants closely regularly, then you will see him before he can become established. They can be picked off by hand and destroyed and the plant sprayed with vegetable soap or neem for good measure.

Another common pest that is more difficult to spot is the spider mite. These creatures are almost microscopic bit their presence will be given away by white spots on the leaves and fine silky webbing on the undersides. Early infestations can be resolved simply by spraying the underside of the leaves with a harsh jet of water. If they persist then use a garlic spray or some neem oil.

The other pest that blights this plant is the flea beetle. These tiny jumping beetles have a similar appearance to fleas and chew holes in the leaves which leave the plant looking like someone had a go at it with a shotgun. A seventy percent neem oil spray will typically deal with infestations if they are caught early. Further, into this book series, we will take a more in-depth look at some of the organic methods for dealing with common garden pests.

CAULIFLOWER:

Cauliflowers are loaded with anti-oxidants and teeming with vitamin C. Despite these health benefits; they languished for many years in the background along with those vegetables that were only eaten occasionally and sometimes even reluctantly. And then came the arrival of the popular low carb diet and suddenly demand for this vegetable went through the roof. Where once the cauliflower had been seen as lacking taste and only edible if smothered in a creamy white sauce, top chefs were now promoting it and offering a wide range of previously unconsidered cooking possibilities. Today this humble vegetable is frequently used as a replacement for the higher calorie potato and is now being served mashed, roasted in a marinade and even barbequed. The ketogenic diet might have knocked the calorie out of fashion, but it certainly placed the cauliflower in fashion.

A member of the brassica family, cauliflowers like a well-fed soil and so will thrive in your raised beds. To ensure a reliable succession, sow seed in March; early May and again in early June. You have the option of sowing directly into the ground or into modules. I would suggest sowing the first two crops in modules and the last directly into the ground when the weather is a bit more reliable. When using modules, sow the seed an inch deep and two to a module. They grow quickly and will be ready to plant out in around four weeks. Where two seedlings appear in a module, select the stronger of the pair and pinch out the other. Don't attempt to pull out the one that doesn't make the cut as you will damage the roots of the plant you want to keep. Plants grown in modules will get leggy if they have too much heat or too much light so grow them on a moderately warm windowsill and keep them damp but not wet.

Like most seedlings started indoors, they will need to be hardened off before planting out. To get really big heads, space your seedlings two feet apart. In the more confined space of a raised bed, you can keep them closer together, but the heads will be smaller. It becomes a matter of personal preference whether you want giant plants or not. Because they are a little sensitive to drying out, it is important to either plant them in the evening or water in straight after planting.

Several pests are attracted to cauliflower and have been since way before the low carb diet came into fashion. Perhaps the fact that you seldom see an obese cabbage root fly is testimony to just how effective this trendy diet can be. These pesky little creatures look a bit like a house fly but are more of a grey colour. They like to lay their eggs at the base of your plants and when the eggs hatch the maggots crawl down and feast on the roots. The first thing the gardener knows about this is when his plant starts to wilt, and the leaves turn a bluish-grey colour. By then it is usually too late and the plant quickly succumbs.

There are a couple of ways to deal with this that conform to organic principals. The most effective is to cover the plants with fine mesh, sometimes called bio mesh, which denies access to the fly. It is not a very pretty sight, but as long as the mesh is in place your plants are safe.

The second method is to make plant collars. These are simple collars, cut from roofing felt or carpet underlay that fit around the stem of the plant and prevent the maggots from getting to the roots. It is not quite as effective as the mesh method but is far less obtrusive visually. I would suggest that you experiment with both and see what system work best for you.

Another cauliflower connoisseur is the cabbage white caterpillar. These are the progeny of the rather attractive cabbage white butterfly. The caterpillars are green, and there is no such thing as one cabbage white caterpillar. They tend to emerge in thuggish gangs that can decimate the leaves of an entire plant overnight. Close observation is your optimum weapon here. The butterfly lays her yellow eggs in batches on the underside of the leaves and, provided you are looking for them, they are relatively easy to spot. You can then simply rub them between thumb and forefinger, and the whole problem is avoided. This is another one of those instances where raised beds can really make your life that little bit easier. Not having to bend as much makes the egg hunt far less like a Pilates stretch class. If you are using bio netting against the cabbage fly, you will, of course, eliminate this pest at the same time.

The cabbage whitefly is a type of aphid who also does his best to make your gardening life that little bit more of a challenge. Like all aphids, these are sap-sucking insects that inject their tiny proboscises into the leaf and feed on the sap. They secrete a sticky substance politely referred to as honeydew, and this can easily contribute to fungal diseases. Ants love honeydew and will actually farm the aphid by carrying them to different parts of the plant. Often it is the ant that first alerts the gardener to the aphid's presence. Compared to other pests, these guys are wimps and can easily be blasted out of existence with a hose or squirt of vegetable soap. Once you have learned to spot them, you will be able to pick them off before they can become established mercilessly.

Clubroot is a disease that commonly affects cauliflower but is much more of a problem when plants are grown in the open ground than in raised beds. It thrives in infected soil, and as the raised bed soil is normally of such high quality, incidents of it in these environments are far less common. It manifests itself through reddish-purple leaves and weak growth. When the plant is pulled up, there are knobbly lumps on the roots that are a sure indicator as to the causes of this problem. It can be avoided by choosing resistant varieties. If you do have infected plants, they should not be added to the compost, and the top layer of the soil should be replaced.

GLOBE ARTICHOKE:

These are plants that are both delicious to eat and easy to grow. Also, they provide a wonderful architectural element to the garden because of their impressive form. They are perennial, so they don't need to be replaced every year. With all of these attributes going for them, you would think that this was one plant that would be far more widely grown by the home gardener. The reason for the lack of take up is that many people simply aren't sure what to do with them from a culinary point of view, and so they are simply overlooked.

Start seeds off in trays in late March to early April and plant them half an inch deep. As soon as they are large enough to handle, they can be hardened off and moved to their new permanent home. Normally they will have about five or six leaves by then. Bear in mind they are both tall and will be around for some years, so put some thought into where you plant them. If you are lucky, you should get a few flowers at the end of the first year. Don't worry if there are not many, they will go on producing the following year, and flowering will be far more prolific. In autumn; mulch their bases with compost or straw.

These plants are not very prone to pests but keep an eye out for the odd mob of marauding aphids. Blast them off with water or vegetable soap depending on your weapon of choice. When young they are favoured by snails and slugs, but hopefully, the raised bed helps keep these guys in check. Flowers can be simply snipped off in July or August when they are the size of a golf ball. This will give you the first crop and encourage the plant to produce a second. Boil the flower until it is soft enough to easily remove the scale-like leaves and then fry the hearts in butter. It really is that simple and they are delicious.

As they get older, plants become woody and start to produce fewer flowers. Lift them with a garden fork and divide them to encourage new fresh growth. Good varieties include 'Purple Sicilian' and 'Green Globe'.

PARSNIPS:

Parsnips are a popular root crop, but they can be a little tricky. This stems from the fact that, unlike carrots which may look somewhat similar, parsnips must be grown using fresh seed. Purchase seed each season and check the date on the packet to ensure that what you are buying is in date. Generally, you will end up with more seed than you can use and it is very tempting to keep this and hope that you can get a second sowing the following year. The success rate will be so low that you are far better off just giving the seed away to another gardener while it is still viable. One of the main reasons that people believe this to be a problematic crop is that they attempt to use old seed.

Plant seeds about three inches apart in drills that are one inch deep. The seeds are incredibly light, so it is probably best not to try this on a windy day. Cover the seeds and water in lightly. This should be done in early May. One month later when the plants are starting to germinate, thin out every second plant. This ensures that they have plenty of space to grow without competing with one another. If you leave this part of the operation too late, you risk damaging the roots of those plants that you want to keep.

Don't feed them during as this will lead to leaf growth at the expense of the root. The best time to harvest is just after the first frosts of the season. They should lift easily and should be large and healthy.

People planting directly into the ground often plant their parsnips in toilet rolls. This ensures that the gardener gets strong straight growth and the roots aren't diverted when they hit stones or other underground obstacles. By the time the toilet roll disintegrates, the roots are strong enough to push their way past anything that might get in their way. In the raised bed environment, the soil is normally so conditioned that it is not really necessary but feel free to use this technique if you feel your growing medium is too stony.

SWEET POTATOES:

Another delicious garden plant that is only really being discovered by home gardeners. The sweet potato is grown from slips which you can purchase but which tend to be expensive when you can find them. They are so easy to produce yourself that once you have done this, you will wonder why anyone ever buys them.

Mound some of your planting mix to a height of eight inches high and twelve inches wide. Leave three feet between the rows. This means that you can comfortably get two rows in a four-foot-wide raised bed. You can now plant your rooted slips every twelve inches along each of the mounds. Unlike ordinary potatoes, they don't grow as bushes but as sprawling vines. Though they can take up a lot of space and would probably account for a whole bed, they are attractive, especially if left hanging from a vertical planter.

They should be planted out in spring and will be ready to harvest by late summer. The vines will dry out when the potatoes are ready, and you should stop watering at that stage. Leave

194 | ADVANCED RAISED BED GARDENING GUIDE

them dry for the last three weeks before digging them up. They can easily be lifted with a fork but go in wide of the plants to avoid stabbing your crop. Throughout the growing season, they need to be kept evenly moist. This is best done by letting the top two inches of the soil go dry. Test regularly to ensure that though the soil surface is dry but that the subsoil is still moist. You can do this by merely poking your finger two inches into the soil and feeling for dampness.

To produce your own slips, cut one of your potatoes in half and stand it in an old ice cream container with an inch of water in the bottom. Top up the water from time to time so that the base of the potato does not become dry. Stand the container on a windowsill, and after a month you will start to see shoots growing from the sides of your parent potatoes. Once these are around twelve inches high, then simply snap them off the edge of the potatoes and stand each one in a jar of water. All the base of the stem that is submerged will start to produce roots. When the roots are established, then you can pot up your new plant into a pot filled with potting soil. Continue to grow them indoors for another month and then plant them out in May. They will need to be kept under a fleece for the first week or two to harden off safely. You should be able to harvest in November. Expect to get roughly four to six slips per half parent potato.

SWEET CORN:

The next slightly unusual crop we're going to look at is sweet corn. Scientists believe that human beings have been growing corn for the last 10,000 years. It was developed from the grass 'teosinte' in Mexico, although what we eat today is very different from the corn of that era. You will need to make sure when you buy your seed, that you purchase a variety that has been designated as sweet corn. There is corn designed for popcorn, flour and animal feed, and none of these will prove delicious when served on the dining table.

Corn makes up a large part of the staple diet in many parts of the world. Corn, or maize as it is sometimes called, is grown far more widely than either wheat or rice. Although it makes up the staple diet in many places, most production is intended for animal feed and increasingly for ethanol as a fuel additive. In fact, in some parts of Europe, many people are still suspicious of eating corn as a vegetable as they are far more familiar using at it as duck or cattle fodder. This is mainly because they have not encountered the sweeter cultivars of this particular crop. What they have been growing and feeding their livestock for decades, is a tough and unsavoury variety of maize.

Corn is a warm-weather crop. Ideally, it prefers temperatures of between 20 and 30° C. It does not like to drop below 10° C at any time. It is an ideal crop to plant into beds after lettuce or some of your early leafy vegetables. Before planting, lightly dig over the bed with a fork while at the same time digging in some manure or rich compost. Traditionally in parts of the world where corn was widely consumed, it was grown on top of fish carcasses which would have provided plenty of nutrients. The stalks were used as a climbing support for beans and the shade that the plants provided created a cool growing environment for pumpkins. This multi-cropping method is still very much a part of the permaculture movement. Whilst this is still a viable option, I would recommend that you grow your sweet corn in a bed dedicated solely to this crop, at least until you are familiar with it.

When growing corn, it is a good idea to start some off in containers in the house four weeks before it is are due to be planted out in early May. Come May, provided the weather is warm enough, plant out your seedlings, but at the same time plant some seeds directly into the bed to provide a succession crop once you have reaped the first one. Three weeks after you have planted the seeds and the seedlings, you can sow a second crop of seeds. This should provide you with a steady succession of sweet corn throughout the summer season. You need to plant your plants about 12 inches apart. Any closer together than that and the plants will be shading one another and rubbing together, and they will not perform well. Seeds should be planted in rows at a depth of one and a half inches. Sow two or three seeds per hole and then snip off weaker plants once they come through. There's an argument as to whether to grow in blocks or rows. This is because, unlike most crops which are pollinated by insects, corn is wind-pollinated. The pollen is carried on the flowering heads of the male plants. The silky tassel on the cob is the female plant that will need to come into contact with the wind-born pollen to provide fruit on the cob. By keeping your crop in blocks, the argument goes, you increase the chances of the pollen reaching the female plant. I have not found any particular difference in yield, whether in rows or blocks.

Bear in mind that corn cannot withstand cold of any kind and is very thirsty. You will need to water regularly. It does not need to be fed during the growing season but should be planted into any already rich bed. Remember that corn is a grass and the last thing you want is for it to grow tall and leggy which it will do if you give it too much fertilizer. Each succession that you plant should take about 10 to 12 weeks to ripen. Ensure that your last succession isn't still trying to mature when the weather becomes cold.

You can tell when the cobs are ripe because the ends become more rounded and the silk becomes brown. As you reap the last of the ripened cobs from each successive planting, you can remove the stems and leaves and add them to your compost heap. This will allow both space and light for the crops that are following. You do not need to reap all of the cobs as soon as they become ripe. You can leave them on the plant for several days but do not leave them for too long, or they will become floury and eventually dry out.

Whilst corn is a wonderful crop both to eat and to grow; you need to bear in mind that it takes up a lot of space and is very thirsty. It would help if you also considered that because of its height; plants can reach 1.8 meters tall, it will cast plenty of shade which may affect other crops that you wish to grow. Another thing to consider is that corn is a shallow-rooted plant. This means that you consider the wind in your area. If you live in a wind-blown place, you will need to plant your crop in a sheltered position. If you don't, the wind might knock your plants down. If you have raised beds that are high, the full-grown plants will be at quite a height. One way to reduce this wind vulnerability will be to use smaller cultivars that remain relatively small though this will result in a smaller yield of cobs.

BROCCOLI:

Over recent years broccoli has gone through something of a renaissance primarily due to its reputation as being a superfood. This is because of its high vitamin carrying capacity and a high content of anti-cancer properties. Although I cannot vouch for its efficacy is a superfood, I do know the broccoli is one of these crops where the homegrown variety is simply far more delicious than anything you will find in the supermarket. What is more, is that supermarket broccoli has become quite expensive and this is an added incentive to produce your own. There are many different varieties of broccoli, and you're going to need to experiment to find out which ones best suit your requirements and growing conditions. Whichever variety you opt for, I recommend that you cultivate and grow them in containers for eight weeks before planting them out. The tender seedlings are just too tempting for slugs and snails to risk sowing directly into your bed.

Sow two seeds per cell and then thin to one once you can see which of the pair is going to be weaker. Keep your seedlings on a windowsill or in a greenhouse until they're about 5 inches high. Once a week you can feed them with a liquid feed so that they are in prime condition when you plant them.

They will need to be planted in a bed that receives full sun or a little bit of shade. You should plant each seedling 1 foot apart in rows 18 inches apart. As soon as they go into the ground, you should cover your seedlings with netting. Being members of the brassica family, these plants are a delicacy to pests such as cabbage butterfly and cabbage fly. You will need to keep them netted in taller plants or until they are well enough established and their leaves are tough enough to resist the threats.

Broccoli produces a healthy head which I'm sure you are familiar with after having seen them in your local supermarket. As soon as the head is large enough cut it off with a knife and it is ready to prepare. If you leave it on the plant for too long, it will turn yellow as each of little buds that make up the head is a flower bud and you need to harvest before the flowers open. Leave the remainder of the plant in the ground, and it will continue to produce smaller sprouts that you can cut off and eat.

The softer leaves that surround the head are perfectly edible and can be treated and cooked in the same way that Kale can. Another trick to make your harvest go further and avoid waste is to peel the hard stem that the head is carried on and cook that in the same way as you would regular broccoli.

One of the common problems that beginners have when growing this vegetable is that they have lovely healthy-looking plants that simply fail to produce a head of any kind. This is most commonly due to the fact that they have not given the plant sufficient water. Broccoli is another of those crops that require a great deal of water to produce well. Bolting can also be an issue, but if you see the head starting to turn yellow, then cut it off immediately. You should be able to collect some edible material from the head but, more importantly, the plant will now start to produce more sprouts, and your efforts won't have been wasted.

Some people sow seed directly into the beds after April. The reason that I don't do this is that the seedlings are so vulnerable to attack by pests. If that is not an issue in your garden, then you might prefer this method than going to all the effort of growing indoors in modules. I would still recommend the use of netting.

Finally, there are many different varieties of broccoli. These include differences in shape, size and colour, but more importantly, differences in timing. You will need to experiment with early and late varieties and see which provide you with the best results. They grow well with Kale which is yet another superfood.

MELONS:

There is something about growing your own melons that just says that you have arrived as a gardener. They are not all that difficult to produce but people always think that they are and is it really your job to correct that misconception? Not only will they give you instant kudos in the word of gardeners, but their fruit also provides one of the most delicious of summer rewards and costs a small fortune when purchased at the local greengrocer.

If you are going to grow melons in a raised bed, then you will want to climb them up a trellis. Something like watermelon can spread 15 feet in all directions and unless the gardener introduces some form of discipline, then a plant this vigorous can soon get out of control. With the ideal conditions that the raised bed provides, an uncontrolled melon will happily make your garden look like into a set from The Day of the Triffids. Also, it is not just what is above ground that is greedy for space. Below ground, the roots will be equally territorial. The trellis is the ideal answer to this problem but melons, and especially watermelons, can be really heavy so that trellis will need to be secure. It should also be high if the watermelon is your melon of choice. Seven feet will be just about high enough.

Melons need plenty of sun, and they have a long growing season. This means you will want to get them into the ground early but well after the last frosts. If you live in an area where the growing season is short and the soil is slow to warm up then cover the soil with black plastic to gain those crucial few degrees. You can also start your melons off in modules, but they are deep-rooted plants so this is not ideal.

The surest way to get a good result is to plant your seed directly into your bed. Unless your bed is enormous, then it is probably best to have one dedicated solely to melons because they like their space so much. That doesn't stop you growing an early crop before the melons go in and another autumn crop once they are harvested so that the bed remains highly productive overall.

Melons have a particularly long growing season as most of them originate in areas where long hot summers are the norm. As you are probably going to be cultivating in areas that are not quite ideal, you should choose your varieties with care. Traditional melons take 90 to 100 days to reach maturity. If you opt for a variety that is quicker growing, you can knock this down to 75 days. Not only will that make reaching maturity more likely, but it will also mean that you get your bed back earlier to sow another crop.

I have mentioned the importance of choosing your varieties with care several times in this chapter. It really can be a game-changer, especially in the raised bed arena where space is sometimes limited but the gardener still wants to maximize yields. Plant breeders have spent decades developing varieties with different traits such as dwarf varieties of maize, late or early broccoli or melons that fruit early. Learning which varieties best suit your needs is essential because it really can make a difference to the yield that you can produce. That is one of the reasons that gardeners spend so long poring over seed catalogues. These can be invaluable when it comes to choosing what to plant. I tend to steer clear of seeds that have just come out and have yet to be proven in the field. Instead, I go for varieties that have been around for some time and have withstood the tests that the market imposes on them. With the advent of the internet, I am now able to research a particular variety and see what other gardeners have experienced. In this way, I am no longer reliant purely on the lyrical marketing descriptions provided by the seed merchant and can get a broader range of opinion.

Melons will need to be tied into the trellis as they grow. They do produce tendrils, but these plants are used to sprawling over the ground, and the tendrils won't hold to the trellis in the same way that peas or runner beans will. A watermelon can grow as much as two feet per week so expect to be doing quite a lot of tying in. I generally let the main shoot keep growing upwards until it reaches the top of the trellis and I pinch out most of the side shoots to prevent things from becoming overcrowded. Don't be in too much of a rush to cut back side shoots. You want to ensure that you have enough flowers to produce fruit so let the fruit start to develop before cutting out side shoots. This will cause more nutrients to go toward the fruit rather than side shoots. Ties will need to be soft because the plant's stems are quite fragile. Instead of using string as you would typically do for this job, consider strips of plastic or old nylon tights.

It is not only the vines that will have to be tied into the trellis. When the plant starts to produce fruit, these too will need to be supported. Every gardener seems to have his favourite system for holding up melons. Common choices include netting, old T-shirts, nylon stockings and voluptuous bras. Quite which method you opt for is down to you, as long as whatever is supporting the melon is tied securely to the trellis. You will need to recognize that your melon is going to gain in both weight and size and the tension that this applies must be suspended by the trellis rather than the vine, which could well break.

Initially, the vine will produce many fruits and it might be tempting to keep them all in the hopes of securing a bumper crop. Unfortunately, life is not so kind. Some of the fruit will wither naturally and some you will need to clip off. Wait a while to see which ones show the most potential and then decide if you want quantity or size. Don't go for more than four fruit per plant as they will not mature well. If you want a giant fruit, then snip off all but one but expect to have to support a very heavy watermelon.

Finally, knowing when to harvest your melons can be a bit of a trick because they all have their distinctive signs to show that they are ripe. Watermelons have a tendril growing on the stem immediately behind the melon itself. Don't break this off because this is the perfect tell-tale as to the fruit's ripeness. When that little tendril curls up and goes brown, you can harvest in safety.

The cantaloupe, on the other hand, will change from green to tan in colour, and this tells you that it is nearing perfection. If you gently tug the fruit and it comes away from the stem, then you are fine. If it doesn't let go without a fight, then leave it on the vine for another day or two.

The honeydew rind will turn from green to white or yellow. Unlike the cantaloupe, it will not come away from the vine easily and will need to be snipped off. It will then continue to ripen in a cool room for the next few days.

KALE:

Kale is one of those vegetables that are not only nutritious but also brings with it an attractive stately appearance. We have been eating Kale from more than 2000 years, and it is another one of those so-called superfoods. Unlike most vegetables, it will tolerate as little as 4 hours of sun per day. It can also be sown directly into your beds 4 to 6 weeks before the last frosts. This plant takes eight or nine weeks to reach maturity. If you want to eat it raw in salads, then you can snap off a few of the younger leaves earlier than that.

Seeds should be planted half an inch deep and 12 inches apart. Once they have germinated then mulch the ground with compost and feed the plants once per month with compost tea. They need to be well watered once per week in dry conditions.

This plant is from the same family as broccoli, and many gardeners choose to grow these plants together. Part of the reason for this is that both plants are susceptible to the same pests, these being cabbage caterpillars and cabbage fly. As the two plants go well together and as they are both attacked by the same pests, it makes sense to grow them in the same bed because then you can net both plants at the same time. They also share the same growing requirements. If you do decide to grow these two plants together, make sure that you opt for varieties that will reach a similar height. If you don't do this, the taller plant will dominate and steal from the smaller one.

Kale leaves can be very tough, and although the younger leaves can be eaten raw, mature leaves will need to be cooked. There are a variety of ways of doing this including frying them as chips as a replacement for the potato chip or adding them to stir-fries, soups and stews. The centre stems will need to be removed because they tend to be extremely tough and are almost inedible. Kale can be stored in a plastic bag in the refrigerator with most of the air squeezed out of the bag. If the leaves start to turn yellow, then it is probably time you added it to the compost heap.

ARUGULA:

This is a wonderful cool weather plant that you may be more familiar with under its common name of rocket. Some gardening books refer to it as roquette but in my opinion, this is just downright pretentious (unless you happen to be reading in French).

This crop will produce profuse amounts of leaves if it is happy, and this, in turn, makes me happy because its sharp spicey leaves really add something to salads. Because it prefers cool conditions, it is best cultivated in early spring or early autumn. It can be sown directly into the ground or started off in containers.

To grow it in the ground, make shallow drills with the edge of a trowel and then sprinkle the fine seed directly from the packet to create an almost continuous row of seed. Rows should be spaced about four inches apart. Cover the seed lightly with soil and then water in gently. Don't bother to thin the seedlings once they appear as this plant can tolerate a bit of crowding and you will probably consume it fairly quickly.

You can also sow seeds in modules and start them off on a sunny windowsill. They will germinate in four to five days.

Plant them out when the first roots start to appear through the bottom of the module.

Once established, the plants will need to be kept moist and not allowed to dry out or they will bolt. As with many cool-weather plants, bolting is something you will need to keep an eye out for. If they do show signs of trying to set seed, then harvest them immediately and you should be able to salvage some edible material.

They only need four to five hours of sun per day, so if you have a bed that gets a little shade, this will be the place to plant them. They are prone to attack from flea beetles which will pepper the leaves with tiny holes. These are still edible but it weakens the plant. To overcome this issue, the easiest and most organically effective way is to cover the plants with netting and only open it up when you are harvesting.

BRUSSELS SPROUTS:

There can be few vegetables that generate more of a like em or hate em attitude than the good old brussels sprout. I won't enter into that debate here other than to say they are a great crop to plant in raised beds but that they can provide challenges for the gardener. They need a long growing season, and they tend to be top-heavy so you will need to provide them with stakes. To further complicate matters, they like to be kept moist, and they don't like the weather to be too warm. If you are not a true fan of this vegetable, I suspect that you are already seeing this plant as having enough get-out clauses for you to ignore them altogether.

Challenging though they may be, they are still worth the effort. They are high in vitamins for starters. A small handful of them contains more vitamin C than four oranges, and they store well. Because of their long growing season, you will almost definitely need to start them off indoors or undercover somewhere. Once your seedlings are established, they can be planted out, but they will need to be kept about eighteen inches apart. Get your stakes in early, so you don't risk damaging the root system at a later stage.

Most gardeners plant seed in mid-March indoors and then get them into the ground by early May. This allows them to get established before the hotter weather really sets in. As members of the brassica family, they are prone to attack from the usual suspects; the cabbage white butterfly and the cabbage fly. Net them as soon as they go into the ground as they are at their most vulnerable. Another thing to remember about all members of the brassica family is that they like plenty of nitrogen. If you have been managing your beds well, this shouldn't be an issue but try not to plant them in beds that have just produced a brassica crop.

They can be grown with cabbage as the two plants have similar growing requirements and the difference in heights make them ideal growing partners. As they become taller some of the lower leaves can be removed. This encourages the plant to direct more nutrients towards the sprouts and also facilitates air and light getting to them. One tip is to cut the lower leaves before they get too tough and then they can be cooked and eaten like cabbage.

Continue removing the lower leaves with either secateurs or a knife as the plant grows. It really only needs a clump of leaves at the top to be able to photosynthesize effectively. As they are heavy feeders, give them a watering with nettle tea or liquid fish food every three weeks and keep them well mulched with compost. They require 110 to 120 days to get to a stage where they are ready for harvest and often this will take place only after the first frosts have struck. It is widely believed that this early frost exposure improves the taste of the sprouts.

The lower sprouts will reach a harvestable size earlier than those higher up the plant, but they can be harvested gradually so those higher ones will have time to reach a better size. Some plants may produce relatively small sprouts. If you snap off the top two inches of the plant, the sprouts should grow larger. That top piece that you snap off can be cooked and is one of the most delicious parts of the whole plant.

If you are living in a warm climate, then the best time to plant them out is in early autumn. Look for a winter growing variety as these will be hardier. This will generate a late winter harvest. They can withstand frost, so they make a good winter crop. Just before the first frosts, pinch out the top inch or two of the growing stems. Again, this will encourage the plant to focus its growth lower down and will result in larger sprouts. A good harvest would see you getting approximately fifty sprouts per plant.

With a winter crop, you will be able to remove the netting as soon as the weather cools and the pests go into retreat.

KALETTES:

In the world of superfoods, kalettes are the new kid on the block. There are now so many of these so-called superfoods that if you are growing them all you might want to think about wearing a cape. Kalettes are a cross between brussels sprouts and Kale. Instead of the sprouts springing out up the stem of the plant, you will find small florets which look like miniature kale plants. They are grown in very much the same way as brussels sprouts with all of the same growing requirements though they require less space. Like brussels sprouts, they come in different varieties, and you will need to choose one that corresponds with your growing temperatures and the time of year that you wish to plant.

Once the small florets of leaves are harvested, they can be cooked and treated as winter greens. Those that are not brussels sprouts fans will be pleased to know that the taste is more like Kale than it is like sprouts.

With both brussels sprouts and kalettes, once you have harvested, cut off the plant at the base of the stem and allow what is still below ground to decay back into the soil where it will simply add to the richness of the soil.

OTHER FRUIT:

During the course of this book and its predecessor, much of the focus of raised bed gardening has been toward the production of vegetables. This system indeed lends itself to growing vegetables, but I like to think of the raised bed garden as being a more holistic production zone. Many gardeners today, are trying to reach a point where they are as self-sufficient as possible. In order to do this, we need to think about fruit as well as vegetables. Whilst melons may be something of a luxury; there are plenty of other fruits that can be produced by the home gardener that will increase his productivity and self-sufficiency. Although much of this fruit is not really dependent on their raised bed system, planting fruit trees and bushes may still be something you want to consider when you design your garden.

Later in this series, we will be looking at fruit in greater depth, but at the moment, I simply want you to understand that there is room in the raised bed garden system to incorporate fruit. Cane fruits such as blueberries, thornless blackberries, raspberries and red currants all thrive in raised beds, but you can go further than that. The worry most beginner gardeners have is that tree fruits such as apples, pears and quince will get too big for the space allotted to them and cast shade over the raised beds.

It is entirely possible, to purchase and plant dwarf varieties of fruit or to train your fruit trees to grow along wires in a system that is known as espalier cultivation. Using this system, the branches of the chosen tree would be tied onto support wires that run along a fence, for example. The fruit tree is then rigidly disciplined to grow and produce fruit parallel to the fence and does not need to impinge on the space allotted to the raised bed section of the garden. Done correctly, this can also become a beautiful frame for any garden. As an alternative to the regular espalier system, both pears and apples can be trained as stepovers providing the correct varieties are chosen. A stepover fruit tree is one that is trained to grow along a low wire and produce fruit at the height of little more than one foot.

All of these options that we will look at in more depth later in the series. I mention it at this stage merely to encourage you to think or your raised bed garden as being more than just for the production of vegetables.

5

EXTENDING THE GROWING SEASON

*I*n both this book and its predecessor, An Introduction to Raised Bed Gardening, I have touched on the subject of self-sufficiency. I have been careful to point out that these methods might lead you toward self-sufficiency. Going fully self-sufficient is a far more complicated matter. Growing all of your own fruit and vegetables is demanding work and a more realistic aspiration would be to produce the majority of the fruit and vegetables that you and your family consume. There is a reason for this, and it affects even the most dedicated gardeners.

The lean season or the hungry gap, are terms used to refer to that period between late winter and early summer. It is that punitive time where you have consumed all of the produce you stored, canned and froze the previous year but before you are able to harvest anything from the current season. It is not a new phenomenon and it has blighted gardeners and farmers since we first started to sow the seed to soil.

Producing crops twelve months of the year is difficult and becomes something of a juggling act that can really test a gardener's skills. It is, however, gratifying pulling something edible from the ground at a time when the earth appears barren and devoid of nourishment. In this chapter, we will be looking at some of the tricks to prolong the growing season. I am still not promising that you will never need to venture into the greengrocer's again, but you will be in a position to maximise the productivity of those raised beds that you worked so hard to install. I always think it is a shame when I see beds lying fallow that could, with a little effort and ingenuity, be producing something useful for the kitchen. Lean season beds may not be the lush eye-catching affairs that they are in the gentler months, but they can still deliver healthy produce.

To maximise your yield, you are going to need to get the hang of the different varieties of vegetables available. Many of them will have attributes that can dramatically extend the growing season. Seed merchants and nurserymen will often offer varieties that are early producers, late producers or are hardier than the more familiar seeds and vegetables that we commonly use. This can open the door to producing crops outside of what we consider the normal seasonal range. Many gardeners ignore these seeds because they have their traditional favourites or because they have become used to growing certain plants at a specific time of year. A gardener only has to pay attention to what is printed on the seed packet or in the catalogue to discover a whole new world of seeds that can vastly increase annual yields. To add to this, we are now blessed with access to a vast treasure trove of information via the internet, and it is worth starting to become familiar with tapping into this resource.

For the gardener wanting to maximise his harvest, planning becomes essential. You will need to know in advance what crops are going to go into the ground when, and at what time they are going to be harvested. Once these plans are fully developed, the gardener will be able to harvest and then plant successively so that the beds are never being left in an unproductive state. Obviously, there might be slight hiccups in these plans due to weather and environmental factors, but by and large, the gardener will have a good idea of what will be happening and when. Raised beds greatly facilitate these opportunities because the gardener is so easily able to ensure that the soil is always in tip-top condition.

A well-developed garden plan will include what seeds or plants are going into the ground and when and what varieties they are going to be. It will also incorporate what seedlings are growing in the house or greenhouse. There was a time when creating garden plans of this depth and detail would take a gardener days or even weeks of in-depth research and study. Today there are easy to use apps that take much of the hard work out of this vital job. Despite this, however, the gardener is still going to have to build up their own knowledge because no app or planning book is going offer the kind of information that actual hands-on gardening provides.

At the end of the planning process, you should come away with a month by month garden plan, which you would be well advised to print out. That way you can not only refer to it regularly but also make notes so that the following season you will have a road map of where you are going and what did and didn't work the previous season. Over time, you will build up a wealth of knowledge which will prove invaluable to you as a gardener. No book or app will ever be able to provide the kind of in-depth information specific to your garden that this experience will. The only other way to short cut this system is to beg, steal or borrow information from more experienced gardeners in your local area. Many new gardeners can be a little shy about doing this, but I can't reiterate enough how much I was helped by older hands when I was starting. Other growers were never reluctant to share their knowledge and experience, and I am certainly happy to pay it down the line to any new gardeners that I can help.

In-depth records and the use of different varieties is an excellent place to start extending your growing season, but other tricks can, and should, be brought into play. Two of the most effective of these are succession and relay planting.

These two techniques can be a little challenging to tell apart at first because they are so similar so let me clarify because these will be terms that you come across frequently. Relay planting is where you plant a different crop in the same space immediately after having removed the first crop. Successive planting is where you plant the same crop in a different space and at a different time, usually a few weeks after the previous one. The idea being that the first sowing ripens and can be harvested before the second sowing reaches maturity.

Both methods are designed to maximise yields by being able to use the available ground for the longest time possible. Here is where experience is really going to start to count. It is tempting to simply print down a chart from the internet or a garden manual and on the date suggested, to plug in the next crop or the next batch of seeds. Oh, if life were only that easy. The growing conditions are what will determine when the next crop can and should go in.

For example, if you want to get your spinach going really early, you plant your first early variety seeds as soon as the soil can be worked. Most charts will advise you to plant the successive crop two weeks later. That is fine in principle, but if the weather has been cold and the first sowing has not emerged from the ground, the second sowing is likely to ripen at exactly the same time, and you will have a glut of spinach that would make Pop Eye draw a sharp breath.

I wish that I could simply offer a magic formula that would overcome this but there isn't one. Though there is a successive sowing chart further into this chapter, please use it more as a guideline than a definitive process. You as the gardener will need to read the conditions in your garden and decide when the time is right to sow successive crops. It is usually preferable to have a few days between crops ripening than to have too much at any one time as this quickly gets out of hand and leads to waste.

Many of the leafy vegetables make ideal crops for succession planting. Spinach can be sown very early using an early variety and then, by switching to later varieties will continue to give yields right up until late summer or early autumn. If this is then followed with a hardy variety over the winter months, and allowed to grow through a protective layer of straw, you should see a yield in early spring. That is right in the middle of the hungry gap. A similar process can be applied to kale, lettuce and broccoli.

An example of good relay plants is to start off with early potatoes and then switch to bush beans as soon as they have been lifted. If you follow a heavy feeder like corn with runner beans that trap nitrogen in the soil, you not only have a relay crop but you improve your soil at the same time.

The use of other methods can enhance both relay and succession methods. Starting seeds off in containers and then having them already established as soon as the weather is kind to you can dramatically lengthen the growing season. That method is not just restricted to the first planting of the year. Your succession crops can be grown indoors and then planted out only when the previous sowing is established. In this way, those plants growing in containers can be kept indoors for a few extra days if the weather is not to your liking.

Although starting seeds off in the house has obvious advantages, there are usually only so many windowsills that you can fill with seedlings without finding yourself in divorce court. The Rolls Royce of alternatives is to have a greenhouse where you can start seedlings, shelter plants that aren't hardy, start cuttings and generally have a good time. There is no getting away from the fact that greenhouses can be an expensive investment and that will need to be weighed up in relation to the returns you can expect from your garden. We will look at greenhouse gardening later in this series, but if you have access to one or are good with your hands, then this is an investment that will definitely open up a whole new range of gardening opportunities.

Greenhouses can be heated using a variety of different methods, they are the ideal place to have built-in hotbeds, and they provide a sheltered space for the gardener to carry on working during those cold winter months.

They are, however, not totally perfect despite the heavy promotion that I have just given them. They need to be kept almost clinically clean in order not to prove a breeding ground for pests and fungal diseases, and they invariably need to be maintained because the woodwork is exposed to warm damp conditions that are so conducive to wood rot.

Even if that dream greenhouse is beyond your financial means at the moment, there are always cheaper options to consider. As a matter of fact, there can be few areas of human endeavour where cheap alternative options are explored as widely as they are in gardening. In general, we gardeners tend to be a tight-fisted bunch.

Cold frames are simple frames, generally made of timber, over which a transparent lid is fitted. This allows plants to grow in a sheltered position much like a greenhouse but for considerably less cost. My frames are made of cheap scaffold boards, and the lids are glass fridge doors that were recovered from a tip. They may not be the most attractive feature of my garden, but they have proved very useful and have been worth every penny of the two pounds that I invested in them. Other cold frames can be made of wood with plastic or a sheet of ordinary glass as the roof. The only thing you will need to consider is how much weight that lid can hold if it snows. Even if you don't want to shell out for a wooden frame, a sheet of glass or plastic over a frame made of blocks positioned in a square or rectangle will do the trick. A cold frame is always going to be limited by the number of plants that it can hold, but owning one can add considerably to the number of plants you can protect and thus prolong your growing season.

Cloches are glass covers that can be stood over an individual plant to help protect it from the cold. Cloche is the French word for a bell, and the French were indeed the first gardeners to use these particular items to cover plants during winter. Today, French cloches can cost a small fortune. They do look rather chic but when its minus 5°C outside and the ground is covered in mud do you really care? You can achieve the same result by cutting the top off an empty plastic drinks bottle. In fact, if you lean two sheets of glass together to form an A-frame, these will do the same job as an imported cloche. The main point to take away from this is that by providing any sort of protection through which the light can penetrate, you will help keep many plants warm enough to extend the growing season.

Tunnel farming, now often referred to as plasticulture, has so changed agriculture that in many parts of Europe we can eat crops such as tomatoes all year round. Raised beds make putting up hoops very easy and when a sheet of strong, clear plastic is attached to this, you in effect, create your tunnel. Inside that tunnel, the temperature will be several degrees warmer than outside. Very often, a few degrees can mean the difference between a seed germinating and not germinating. It also adds that bit of extra growing time that might help a plant ripen earlier or go into the bed earlier. When it comes to increasing yield and extending the growing period, something this simple could make all the difference.

We touched briefly on floating mulches earlier in this series. A floating mulch is a covering of clear plastic or light permeable fleece that is pegged down over a bed to help protect from the cold. It is cost-effective and straightforward, and even the pegs can be made from simple pieces of wire bent to make staples. When you cover a crop of any kind with a floating mulch, then always make sure that you leave enough room for the plant to grow. On warm sunny days, you can uncover the crop and then cover again before nightfall. That way, the soil will benefit from the sun's warmth and the heat will, at least partially, be trapped when the cover is pegged back in place.

Many crops are winter hardy. Garlic, for example, is planted in autumn and will then grow away quite happily during the winter and be ready to harvest early the following spring. The book on winter gardening in this series will deal with this subject in greater depth. At the moment what I am keen for you to know is that you can grow food in your raised beds every day of the year. Lettuce, onions, kale, peas, radishes, spinach and chard are all plants that can be winter grown and which will help eliminate the hungry gap.

There are even some advantages to be gained from growing crops over the winter. There is generally very little need for water during the winter period. I switch off my irrigation system altogether during the colder months and only if it has been really dry will I give a light watering with a hose and wand. It is possible to purchase an irrigation attachment that detects when it has not rained for some time and which will then allow the water to come on. I prefer not to use this as the risk of frost damage to the irrigation system outweighs the advantages of not having to check how dry the soil is from time to time. That test simply consists of me sticking my finger into the soil to the depth of the second knuckle. If I can't feel moisture, then it is probably time for a light targeted watering.

Another significant advantage is that there are far fewer plant pests during the winter than there are at other times of the year. Even slugs and snails seem to go into hibernation, and some of the leafy crops that I harvest are the best that I will reap all year round.

The main crop harvested during winter and early spring will indeed be green leafy vegetables. If you are not a fan of these like I am, then that may seem a little disappointing. Green leafy vegetables are some of the plants most lacking in the modern diet, so you may be able to console yourself with that thought. Another is that these vegetables always seem to become more expensive during winter, so the money you save in relation to what you might have had to buy in also increases.

Finally, we come to the subject of storing our harvest. In gardening terms, food storage is something of a neglected art. Gardening, after all, is all about growing things, getting dirty and wearing muddy boots. Food storage usually takes place in the kitchen and therefore is a totally different subject. If you really want to benefit from the bounty of your garden, then how you preserve what you grow is as important as gardening itself. It certainly is if you want to become as near as possible to being self- sufficient in vegetable production. Good gardeners always experience periods of feast or famine. Poor gardeners only experience the famine.

Those periods of almost glutinous productivity need to be harnessed. We can give away much of the excess in the hope that the neighbours will like us and forgive the fact that we dress badly and always seem to have dirty hands, but that won't feed us during the lean periods.

When I first started gardening, I was very uninterested when it came to preserving my produce, so I empathise with this viewpoint. I have, however, come to find preserving in all its many different forms, to be a gratifying part of the food production process. There is something profoundly rewarding about seeing row upon row of full mason jars on the pantry shelf and having a freezer brimming with beans, peas and carrots that brings out the hunter-gatherer in me. Knowing that I have enough food to live on for months and that it is all the result of my own labours provides a primitive sense of security, even if the mason jars are made of modern glass, and the freezer is powered by electricity.

If you get serious about growing your produce, then the freezer is your best friend. You will be amazed at how quickly you can fill up a big chest freezer throughout a season, and this is crucial to getting through those hungry months when the garden is less productive than it is typically.

You can freeze most vegetables. Some people like to blanch them in boiling water first, but I don't bother and, to be honest, if your garden is in full swing, you probably won't have the time. Beans I simply wash, top and tail and then freeze as soon as they are dry. I place then in a plastic bag and squeeze out the air, and they are good to go. There is a machine that will suck the air out more thoroughly, but it really isn't necessary. Peas I shell, rinse and bag, carrots I usually slice or chop. The only thing that can really go wrong is that you fail to allow the produce to dry before freezing. All that will happen then is that they will freeze into solid chunks that are difficult to get apart when you need to cook them. Even eggplant freezes perfectly after slicing.

Most people will tell you that you cannot freeze tomatoes. This is one crop you can typically be sure of having a glut of, and because freezing is so quick and easy, I was obliged to come up with a method for doing this. I scrape out the inside of the fruit and then turn the shells upside down to drain off some of the juice. I then freeze the shells, and when I need them, I make stuffed tomatoes by merely placing my stuffing directly into the frozen shell before popping it into the oven. The inside I place in a plastic container and freeze as well. When I make the stuffed tomatoes, I defrost the inside flesh and turn it into a sauce.

For potatoes, pumpkin and squash, I chop them along with some onion and freeze them in a plastic bag. When I need to make a soup in the winter, I have one already made, and I remove the bag from the freezer and cook it in a pot with water and seasoning.

All berries, plumbs, red fruit and figs I freeze on a plastic tray. Once they are frozen, I knock them off the tray and throw them into a bag which I throw back into the freezer. They will be fine for crumbles, tarts and smoothies when needed. Apples and pears, I usually freeze only after peeling and coring, but other than that, I use the same method as for other fruit. Frozen apples or pears are fine for crumbles and pies.

Bottling is my next go-to method for storing excess production. This is a little more complicated. For this to work well, you are really going to need mason jars. These you will probably have to buy, but they should pay for themselves within one season. Wash and prepare your produce and pack them into the mason jars. After that cover with salted boiling water, close and ster-ilise in a large pot of boiling water. Sterilising vegetables is just a matter of covering the mason jars with water in a large pot and boiling. Times vary from vegetable to vegetable, and you should check before making your preserve. If you have included meat into the preserve, then you will need to extend that sterilising time to two hours.

There are two types of mason jar. One comes with a glass lid and a rubber seal. The other comes with a two-piece metal lid. I have no particular preference, but some people swear by one or the other so you will want to experiment a little. You will need to sterilise the jars before filling, but this is just a matter of placing them in a pot of boiling water. When you are ready to add the vegetables, remove them from the boiling water, shake off most of the excess water and you are good to go.

If you are using jars with the two-piece metal lid, it is a good idea to let them cool down after sterilising with the vegetable in and then unscrew the outer metal ring of the lid. The inner lid will stay in place because it has been vacuum-sealed by the heat. Dry the outer ring and replace it. This will ensure that any water that crept in does not rust the metal.

These two methods alone will enable you to preserve much of your harvest. Another method that I use when I am pressed for time is the ratatouille method. I fry up onions, garlic, peppers, eggplant, courgettes and tomatoes and season well. For good measure, I might toss in some black olives. Once cooked this mixture can be either frozen or preserved in mason jars. All I then need to do is warm it up when needed, and it is an ideal way to store large quantities of vegetables all at once. Over a day, I might make enough ratatouille to last for a year, and it is a profoundly comforting feeling seeing all those ready-cooked meals lining up the shelves of the pantry.

Jam is another storage method that is very easy and which will prolong the life of your harvest. Don't think this only applies to fruit. Pumpkin, tomatoes and squash can all be turned into jams, either combined with fruit or on their own. Once you start delving into the exotic art of jam, making you will be amazed at the broad spectrum of recipes available.

Here you don't need to go the expense of buying bottles. Simply collect jars from supermarket purchases or ask you less self-sufficient friends to do so. Boil both the jars and the lids in boiling water for ten minutes. Once your jam is ready, remove the jars from the water but not the lids. Place the hot jam into the jars, remove the lids from the hot water and fit them immediately, then turn the bottles upside down to cool. You can store that jam for years.

Other vegetables will store for months without needing to go to such lengths as boiling or freezing. Pumpkins kept in a cool dark place have a very long shelf life. To extend this, stand them on some straw and always make sure not to bruise them during the harvesting process. Carrots can be plunged into dry sand with just the green tops sticking out. These too will last right through the winter. Many varieties of apple can be wrapped in newspaper and stored on a shelf in a cellar or cool dark cupboard. Don't let them touch one another, and their shelf life will carry them well into winter.

Garlic and onions can last a long time if they are kept dry though both of them can be pickled in vinegar, which means they can be kept virtually indefinitely. Many vegetables lend themselves to pickling including cucumbers, onions, mushrooms and cabbage. Cabbage is also made into sauerkraut, and that subject has become so popular in recent years that it has become almost a cult movement.

Fruits such as raspberries, strawberries, red currants and melons can also be preserved in syrup or alcohol. All of these methods not only prolong the life of your produce, but they also add variety and colour to your diet. None of these are tasks that you will master overnight. Instead, they tend to be learned over time and in accordance with where the most abundance occurs in the crop yield. With each new method mastered, the less of a threat the hungry season becomes. Eventually, you reach a point that your preserved stocks are so large that they will not only carry you through the season immediately ahead but possibly even the season after that. Suddenly, self-sufficiency in both fruit and vegetables no longer seems just a romantic notion.

6

ADVANCED SOIL ENRICHMENT

*W*hilst crop management will always be important; it will never reach its true potential unless it is riding on a foundation of good soil management. It is vital to grasp that soil stewardship lies at the heart of all good gardening. Right from the start of this series, we have tried to instil that a gardener's crop can only be as good as the growing medium that goes into those raised beds. In this chapter, we will try to build on that foundation, because it is here that so many gardeners stumble.

When you first started your raised beds, you may well have been so keen to get planting that you took some shortcuts at the soil preparation stage. I know that I did. I purchased soil from someone that may have held his wallet in higher regard than he did my future garden production. He was a swimming pool maker, and he was as eager to sell me topsoil as I was to buy it.

The net result was that much of the soil I bought might not have been topsoil. Instead of a healthy life-giving base filled with living organisms, what I ended up purchasing was more of a desert wasteland. I was just too inexperienced to recognise this at the time. There was enough zest in that soil to give me a good first crop, but after that, the decline was so noticeable that even in my eagerness, I was forced to recognise that I had been somewhat had.

As it turned out, the experience I gained from revitalising the soil and bringing it back to full health has served me well, and so it became just another one of life's little lessons. It could easily have caused a new gardener to decide he lacked the green fingers required to garden successfully and so give up altogether becoming just another supermarket supporter.

What I came away with, and what I hope you too will learn from my misfortune, is that soil can be transformed. It is a substance that is almost eager to resume its role as a material that can sustain life. Providing what you have put into your beds is not actually toxic waste from some nuclear plant, there is a good chance that with a little tender care and patience, you can bring it back to health.

No matter how good soil is, regardless of whether it is encased in a raised bed or you are planting into open ground, the soil will become degraded simply through having nutrients drawn from it by successive crops. When man first began the transition, from hunter-gatherer to farmer, he did not understand this and as a result, was forced to move on every few seasons as the soil became degraded or too heavily populated by pests or diseases. We see the same thing happening in the amazon where forests are burned down and planted but where the soil will only sustain crops for one or two seasons. If those farmers had a better understanding of good soil stewardship, then we might not find ourselves in a place where hundreds of thousands of acres of forest were being burned each year.

Raised beds are basically containers, and a gardener can simply replace the soil inside of them every few years, though at some cost in terms of both labour and finance. With good soil management, the need to change the soil is eliminated. Instead, an ongoing refreshment takes place that is far less costly and much more environmentally sustainable. If this sounds like it might be complicated, then look at the forest as an example. With no added nutrients, the forest manages to sustain some of the largest plants on earth. It does this by continually revitalising the soil with dead plant material in an ongoing process that never stops. Those massive and healthy trees do not need chemical fertilisers or fancy enrichment systems, and yet they thrive.

COMPOST: PROTEIN POWDER FOR YOUR GARDEN

My first choice for bringing soil to optimal health is compost. As you will have gathered as you have read through these books, I am a great believer in compost. It is, in my opinion, the bodybuilding tonic that every garden needs to reach optimal performance. It is natural, easy to produce and free. What is more, is that it is made from materials that would generally go to waste. It is a perfectly balanced nutrient supply, a soil conditioner, a mulch, and it helps retain moisture. How much more can you ask of a free product than that?

Over recent years compost has gone through something of a renaissance as gardeners, businesses and individuals have woken up to its potential. In part, this has been fuelled by the green movement as they have fought to encourage people to move away from synthetic chemical fertilisers and rediscover this wonder material that has always been at our fingertips. I say rediscover because compost is one thing that gardeners have been using effectively for millennia. The widespread use of chemical substitutes really only gained traction after World War II.

Because compost promotes microbial balance, it does not just feed the plants, but the whole mini-ecosystem that exists in healthy soil. A well-balanced soil becomes a sort of living organism in its own right.

The most significant disadvantage of compost is time. Because it is a naturally occurring material, it takes time to make and time for the nutrients and microorganisms to build up to create a balanced soil environment the gardener so desires.

Man has become incredibly impatient recently, and this is a trait that fell straight into the hands of the synthetic fertiliser industry. Why wait for your soil to develop when with one quick application, you can supply the exact nutrients that the plants were lacking. This argument was incredibly powerful when sold to the agricultural industry. They had been practising monoculture on an ever-increasing scale, and this was a sure-fire way to denude soils of specific nutrients. Fertilisers overcame that deficiency in one fell swoop.

The problem with the quick fix solution is that it created a cycle of dependency. Each year fertiliser would be added to the soil to replace that absorbed by the crop, and each year the natural soil ecosystem would be depleted. To add to the problem, whilst it was possible to ensure that enough chemicals were supplied to meet the needs of the plants, it was challenging to know whether too much was being applied and what was happening to the excess. We now know that excess fertiliser use is having a catastrophic effect on the environment.

With nitrogen products alone, we pour 120 million tons onto our fields each year and half of that leaches into rivers and from there makes its way to the ocean. What this results in is algal growth which creates dead zones which cannot support life. This is not some small-scale issue either. Last year the dead zone in the Gulf of Mexico reached 8,800 square miles in size. I don't know about you, but I don't want to participate in the production of toxic tides and dead rivers; especially when there is a far healthier alternative available right on my doorstep if I exhibit just a little bit of patience.

Clearly, I am starting to rant here, and rather than keep going until I foam at the mouth, something I could easily do when talking about this subject, why not look at some ways to get your compost production started.

There are many ways to make compost and some are quicker than others. For reasons I don't quite understand, some people have made composting into this hugely complicated procedure that can leave you feeling like you need a degree in chemistry just to produce a few buckets full. What I am going to propose is a far more simple method that has served me perfectly well for years as it did my grandparents before me.

To make good compost, you need four things. Green waste, brown waste, moisture and air. Green waste is derived mainly from plant materials such as grass clippings, household food scraps, prunings and weeds. Brown waste is woodier and can be from cardboard, non-glossy paper, sawdust, dried leaves or woody material. Green waste is high in nitrogen which is the most essential nutrient in plant growth, and brown waste contains carbon.

To speed up the breakdown process, most brown material should be shredded or cut up finely with secateurs. What you are trying to achieve is a dark, crumbly material that is full of microbes and rich in garden worms. This is where compost purists often get into a heated debate. What percentage of green waste should you incorporate to your mix and what percentage of brown? To be honest with you, I don't have the time to sit around, weighing my waste materials and estimating percentages. When I have lawn clippings, they go in, when I have hedge clippings, they go in. If I can score a pile of old bedding straw from the neighbouring farmer, so much the better. I am reasonably sure that I end up with an overall percentage that is around fifty-fifty, but that may be out on any given day, according to what waste I have collected. Some people suggest a fifty-fifty mix; others recommend a one part green waste to three parts brown. How they get any gardening done when they are so focused on these minutiae of composting is beyond me.

If you have too much green waste, the compost will tell you by going sludgy and starting to smell bitter. Too much brown and the breakdown process will grind to a halt. Don't stress about either event. Just add more of whatever ingredient is lacking and the whole heap will soon self-regulate.

The secret to good compost lies in regular turning as this is what adds the air. The more often you turn the heap, the more oxygen it will contain and the more the microbe level will build-up, which in turn will speed the breakdown process. Turning a large compost heap is physical work. I happen to like physical exercise, and my compost making activities have saved me a small fortune in gym fees over the years. If you prefer to take a less physical approach, then make your compost in a large bin and when the bin is full just kick it over and leave the contents on the ground. The air will have been allowed in, and the composting process will continue.

Good compost gets hot. It can easily reach an internal temperature of around 60° Celsius. If your compost is steaming, it is a good sign. It tells you that microbial activity is operating a maximum potential. The less heat, the slower the process, but if you pile green and brown waste together, it will compost eventually, heat or no heat.

You will hear a whole list of things that you should not add to your compost heap. These include newspaper, citrus, eggshells, garden weeds and cooked food. There are various theories behind this advice, but I ignore all of them. Get your microbe level up to the right levels, and your compost heap will digest anything. There is a very well-known YouTube gardener who buried dead chickens and even a dead kangaroo in his garden, within a matter of months, the microbes had broken those carcasses down to the point where they were additional nutrition for the plants.

While I don't advocate scouring the countryside for roadkill or other carcasses, it does prove my point that a compost heap will eventually digest just about anything apart from old cars. Think of your heap as a giant hungry creature living in the bottom of the garden with broad dietary tastes and an indestructible digestive system.

The only things that don't go into my compost are cat, dog or human faeces, and meat or dairy waste. All of these products would, I am sure, would eventually breakdown. I will, however, be handling the compost and even I need to draw the line occasionally. I have done a tour on an industrial compost facility that deals successfully with hotel waste that includes meat and bones on an ongoing basis, and it is possible to buy pelleted human waste as a fertiliser, but I haven't quite reached that point yet. Clippings from evergreens such as Leylandii just take too long to compost, and so does the moss that I rake from my lawn. These go onto the bonfire, and the ash from that later makes its way onto the heap.

I know my cavalier approach will shock those who have spent years advocating a far stricter approach to compost management, but the fact of the matter is that what I do works. There are easy methods to ensure that your compost is progressing well. The first is to smell it. Compost has a sweet smell similar to what you might notice on the floor of a forest. If it smells bitter or like it is fermenting then chances are you have the ratio of green to brown waste too high. Add more brown material, and the situation will soon correct itself, especially if you turn the material in and allow some air to penetrate.

Moisture control will vary greatly depending on what your weather conditions are. If you live in an area with plenty of rain, then you can reduce the water intake by throwing an old carpet over your compost. If you experience dry spells, then you may need to water lightly from time to time. To test for the correct moisture level, simply pick up a handful of compost and squeeze it tightly. No water should drip out of it, and when you open your hand, the compost should have bound together. Heat is another tell-tale sign that things are progressing well, but the real indicator is the presence of earthworms. Turn over a spade full of healthy compost, and it will be teeming with these creatures.

The composting debate continues just as hotly when you delve into what container you should keep your compost in. There is a wide range of options, and they vary from free to very expensive. There are pros and cons to all of them and they all work.

I use a straightforward three-bay system made out of reclaimed pallets. I hammer posts into the ground as support to create a three-walled container using three pallets. Next to that, I add two more containers, but these only need two pallets each as they share a wall of the adjoining container. This leaves me with three containers of about one cubic meter each. I like to start my compost directly on the ground, so I don't lay anything over the base. That earth is, after all, full of healthy microbes that will soon make their way up into my compost.

Once the first container is about half full of a mixture of green and brown waste, I toss it over into the second container and then start filling the first one again. This airs the compost that I began with.

I do the same thing with the second load of compost. As soon as the container is half-filled, I toss it into the second container where it joins the oldest compost. In theory that second container should now be full, but you will be amazed how much the breaking down process reduces the size of the pile. I can do a third and sometimes even a fourth transfer before that middle container is full. When it is, I toss it into the third container. This gives it more air and the compost is now virtually ready to use but can continue sitting there until I am ready for it. In the meantime, container one is steadily filling again, and the whole process has become an ongoing chain production of raw materials in at one end and compost out at the other.

The speed of the filling process varies depending on the time of year and whether I manage to entice any animal bedding out of my neighbours. There is also no strict rule as to how fast the process will take as this is dependent on the materials going in, the weather and how often I turn the mix. Most people suggest that six months is the minimum, but I believe that time can be considerably reduced if you turn the mix regularly. As the compost gets healthier and hotter, it starts to convert new material more quickly.

Of course, you don't need to use my Scrooge-like pallet system. Compost can be made in plastic bins, containers made from ply or galvanised iron or they can be bought purpose-made. It is possible to buy bins that are suspended on a frame and can be turned by simply winding a handle. Whilst this works effectively, for more extensive gardens, it might be too small, and you would then need a series of them to meet the garden's needs. You also don't necessarily need any container and can make a large pile of green and brown layered material that will produce perfectly good compost providing you turn it from time to time. Even if you live in an apartment, you can keep a small bin on the kitchen counter to gather household scraps and then transfer it to a larger bin on the balcony every day or two.

In short, composting is a very natural and straight forward process which can save you a considerable amount of money, benefits the environment, and it will transform the productivity of your raised beds. Don't be put off by people who try to over-complicate this age-old method. Humans have been composting since long before the study of percentages or the advent of the tumbler bin.

Generally, I try to always be at a point where I have at least one container of garden compost that is ready and can be added to my beds as and when it is needed. When I plant a crop, I mulch with compost, when I lift a crop, I dig some compost into the bed as soon as the crop comes out. If I haven't planted a cover crop and the bed is going to be empty over winter, then I cover it in a layer of compost. Suppose the soil in my beds is looking low then I bulk them up with compost. In short, I am continually reinvigorating my soil with compost as often as is feasible.

LASAGNA GARDENING:

Many gardeners use this system when they start their beds, and it is also sometimes called the layering system. It operates in much the same way as making compost does. They start with an inch or two of brown material followed by an inch or two of green waste and build those layers up one after the other until they have filled their beds. They finish with a layer of brown waste that acts as a blanket until the contents of the bed have broken down and are ready to plant. This process of breaking down takes around six months, and you can tell when it is complete because none of the original green or brown material that went into the bed will be recognisable once breakdown is complete.

The depths of the bed don't need to have all broken down as long as the top few inches are sufficiently composted to plant into. In this way, what you are actually doing is making compost but in a raised bed. I prefer to have my compost where I can apply it as and when I need it, but that is down to personal choice. Personally, I don't like a bed to be out of action for months while the breakdown is happening. If I make the mix directly in the bed, I can't turn it and speed the procedure. I also always like to include natural soil as this always contains those microorganisms that are so essential to the speed of the breakdown process. If you go down the lasagna route, then be prepared for the fact that the contents of the bed will shrink dramatically. You can compensate for this by overfilling the bed by quite a large margin.

If I am not applying a cover crop, and the bed is not going to be planted over the winter months, I may apply compost that has not fully broken down as this can take place in the beds and will free up space in my compost bins at the same time. I think this also further demonstrates how much composting and lasagna gardening have in common. They are more or less the same thing but done in different parts of the garden.

OTHER SOIL ADDITIVES.

Compost is cheap and practical, but depending on your situation, you may have access to other products that you can use that will do a similar job or can be used in conjunction with compost.

SPENT MUSHROOM COMPOST:

There used to be a time when if you lived near a mushroom farm, you could get hold of their waste product for free. Mushroom farmers have become a little savvier to what scroungers gardeners can be, and you may end up having to pay for this product now, though it shouldn't be costly. If you do happen to live near a mushroom farm, it is still worth hitching up your trailer and going down there in some worn clothes looking poor and needy. You could well come away with your trailer filled for free. Don't forget to drop off a box full of vegetables at the end of the season to keep the system oiled.

Mushroom compost is usually made from chicken or horse manure mixed with straw or hay and then steam sterilised. The mushrooms are fungi, and they feed on a whole different range of nutrients to vegetables, so the compost that is being disposed of is still brimming with goodness for the gardener and is a wonderful soil conditioner which provides both permeability and aeration qualities.

Ideally, the compost should have aged for a while before you apply it to your beds, but this process has often already taken place at the mushroom farm where it may well have been laying around for months. It can raise the soil alkaline level and so may not be ideal for cane fruits. On the other hand, it will be appreciated by brassicas such as cabbage, kale, broccoli and Brussel sprouts and may decrease the risk of clubroot disease. Early spring is an excellent time to include this product into your beds.

COFFEE GRINDS:

Coffee shops have begun to pop up on every high street over the last two decades, and each of them produces an incredible amount of vegetable waste in the form of coffee grinds. Despite its brown colouring, this waste product should be regarded as green waste rather than brown carbon waste. Most coffee shops will be happy to give it away as there seems to be no commercial value to it at this stage. The problem you will encounter is not so much that they don't want to give it to you, but instead, they don't want to store it while waiting for you to be in a position to collect it. You will need to negotiate a deal whereby you collect it regularly or supply them with some sort of large bin in which they can put it aside.

Coffee grinds come with all sorts of myths attached to them. Some suggest that they are a deterrent to slugs and snails, but tests have shown this not to be the case. Others claim they are detrimental to plants but that is also not true. The most significant risk they pose when used in the raised bed is that they are very fine and therefore, can act a bit like clay in that they bind together. This has the potential to cause water drainage problems. I have never found this to be an issue. Once I have spread a layer across the surface of the bed, I simply rake it into the soil lightly, and that combines it enough that the binding issue ceases to occur. If I manage to get hold of substantial quantities, I add it to the compost heap and let the worms do the mixing. The grinds appear to have no adverse effect on the worms, and I have found no studies that suggest they may have trouble sleeping at night due to the boost in caffeine intake.

FARMYARD MANURE:

Farmyard manure is a precious resource if you can get hold of it. Contrary to popular city perceptions, manure does not smell bad as long as it has had a few months to break down. Ideally, you want it to arrive when it has already had some time to do this, but it is such a valuable resource that you should take it in whatever state you can get hold of it. If there is still a smell to it, then cover it with soil or compost and let it sit for a few months.

Fresh manure is too strong to apply to beds that are going to have crops in them in the near future. It is easily capable of burning their roots. If the manure you receive is fresh then you can layer it into a bed using the layering method and, in a few months, it will have broken down sufficiently to be planted. It provides a high nutrient source as well as improving moisture retention. If you don't have a bed that you want out of action for the months that it will take to break down the manure then simply feed it gradually into the compost heap. You can even simply ignore it for a few months and then apply it to the beds as a top dressing once it has broken down.

GREEN WASTE:

The combination of garden and kitchen will almost inevitably generate large amounts of green waste. It is easy enough to use this on the compost, but it can also go directly into your beds. Kitchen waste, hedge clippings and lawn clippings can all be layered into the bed where they will break down over time. You don't want to do this in beds that are currently planted but rather into beds that will be dormant for a few months so that the breakdown process will have time to take place. When I harvest things such as cabbages or broccoli, I cut them off at soil level and leave the roots to break down where they will add to the health of the soil.

Provided your top twelve inches of soil is already broken down, it is possible to have deeper layers that are still undergoing this process and still plant on top of them. I never find this a very practical approach other than when filling a bed for the first time. Generally, I prefer to add green waste to the compost heap and then use the composted material either as a soil ameliorant or a top dressing. All of that green waste is moisture retentive and serves to build up the microbiome upon which your plants will thrive. There are a few materials such as clippings of Leylandii and moss that take so long to break down that they should not be added to either beds or compost. Weeds, on the other hand, compost perfectly well and, unless they have gone to seed, any weeds I pull out between the rows of plants I will simply leave on the soil surface to breakdown.

ALTERNATIVE NITROGEN SOURCES:

There is any number of other sources of nitrogen that can be added to the raised bed and many of these can be purchased at garden centres where they usually come in bags. These include alfalfa pellets, soybean meal and even pelleted human waste. They can be mixed into the beds, and they will soon break down and become part of the natural feeding system. I always manage to generate or scrounge so much material that I never seem to need to go to the expense of buying in these additives, but you made need to consider them if you are just starting and your garden had not yet started to create enough green material.

CARBON MATERIAL:

As with green waste, brown waste can also be purchased in any number of different forms. These include coir and peat. Sawdust, straw wood chips and even torn up cardboard will do almost the same thing. All of them are high in carbon and are good at retaining moisture which is their primary function.

Leaf mould is one free resource that I believe is hugely under-valued. If you have even just one or two deciduous trees in your garden then, come autumn, you are going to have an abundance of dry leaves and so often people simply burn this excellent carbon source. Indeed, dry leaves are not high in nutrients, but that does not mean they are without merit. Once broken down, leaf mould is a near-perfect soil conditioner, and it has terrific moisture retention capabilities.

I gather my fallen leaves in cages made from chicken wire. There is really nothing sophisticated about these. They consist of four posts driven into the ground with chicken wire attached. Their primary function is to stop the leaves blowing away before they start to break down. Once they have broken down a little and become damp, then their own weight stops them blowing about and they can just be stored in a heap. Most people will tell you that it takes two years to make usable leaf mould, but I always do it in half that time, and the reason for this is that I add a sprinkling of blood meal from time to time and I turn the material regularly. That dramatically speeds up the breakdown process. By the time the first leaves are falling in autumn, the previous year's material has become black and crumbly. I can add it to my beds, use it as a mulch or simply boost my compost with it. If It took two years to get to a usable state, then I would need twice as many cages. Using my system, the cages I have are empty just in time to fill with the next leaf fall.

IMPROVING DRAINAGE:

So far, all the materials we have looked at have been aimed primarily at increasing moisture retention and adding or replacing nutrients. There may be occasions where you are more interested in increasing the drainage of your beds because they are retaining too much moisture. If you have created a healthy growing medium, this should be quite rare, and you may need to first look at other reasons that the beds are becoming boggy. It could be that the beds are sitting on a material such as clay that is not allowing water to escape or it could be that the sides of the bed are holding the water in too much. Both of these instances are physical factors rather than being a problem related to the growing medium itself. If that is the case, you may need to dig drainage trenches or even drill holes into the sides of the beds.

If the growing medium you have created is high in clay, then drainage might be slow, and you may need to do something about it. Usually, this is rare because as the clay is combined with other green and brown layers, it naturally loses its binding capacity and becomes more free draining. You can hurry this up a bit by mixing sharp sand into the soil. The larger sand granules open up spaces within the clay and over time drainage will be improved. It is a good idea to wash the sand before mixing it into the soil. Both sea sand and building sand can contain minerals that can be harmful to plants.

The other alternative is to purchase vermiculite which is a material made from crushed organic rock. It is chemically neutral and is very good at assisting drainage. It can be purchased at most garden centres but is generally intended for use as an additive to potting soil. On a large scale such as a raised bed garden, it can be quite an expensive way of solving a water retention issue.

COAL DUST:

Another soil intervention that you still sometimes hear of is the addition of coal soot or crushed charcoal to the surface of the soil. This idea dates back many years to a time when Victorian gardeners applied these materials to their beds to cause them to heat up a little earlier in the season. This was mainly done in areas where winters were long and summers were short. The black dust would trap heat, and a few extra degrees could be gained, thus prolonging the growing season.

You still hear of this method being used from time to time, but the advent of black plastic sheeting has almost entirely wiped it out. If you live in an area where winters seem to go on forever, you could cover the surface of your beds with black plastic sheeting. Providing it is tucked in well it will trap heat, and the ground will become workable slightly earlier. A better result might be obtained by applying a thick mulch of dark compost though if there was a great deal of rain, the heat retentive benefits might be offset by the water.

COVER CROPS:

Cover crops are another easy and effective way to keep your beds in pristine health. They are easy to grow and offer many advantages. They suppress weeds, increase organic matter, recycle soil nutrients and retain moisture, so there is little not to like about them. The only reason I can see for not using cover crops is that you are going to grow vegetables all year round.

All year production is a great aspiration, but many people simply don't want to be gardening in the cold and wet, especially if they don't get back from their day job until after dark. Even if you do manage to keep most of your garden in full-time production, there are probably going to be one or two beds sitting idle and here is where cover crops can be of great benefit.

There are hundreds of cover crops to choose from, but they fall into two main categories. Legumes include plants such as vetch, soybeans, clover and peas. It is important to understand that you are not growing them for harvest but as a cover crop. You will not be allowing them to reach full crop bearing maturity. This family of crops are nitrogen binding, so they are reinforcing the nutrient level of your soil.

The second group are grain crops such as rye, oats and wheat. Although they don't have the same nitrogen binding capacity, they break down easily and therefore can be readily dug back into the soil when they are cut back.

Most cover crops grow quickly. Spread the seed of your chosen crop evenly and then rake the soil lightly and water in. If you still have a crop in the ground, like cabbages, for example, you can get the seeds started and have the cabbages harvested before the cover crop is at a size which will impede the cabbage.

The important thing with most cover crops is not to let them set seed; otherwise, you will have to deal with self-set seedlings popping up amongst your crop the following season. The best and most effective way of avoiding this is to cut the crop down as it starts to flower. This also happens to be the time when the plant is most loaded with nutrients which you will now be returning to the soil. You can mow the crop down with a lawnmower or strimmer, cut it down with hedge clippers or dig it over with a fork. The fallen plant material can then either be dug into the bed or simply left lying on the surface where it will break down naturally. Whichever method you opt for, expect about two months for the plant material to break down to a point where the bed is ready for planting.

All of these methods are good for maintaining the structure, microbial life and water retentive capacity of your soil. Although feeding with liquid organic fertilizers such as nettle tea and some of the others we have mentioned, there is nothing that can quite match an overall healthy soil. I urge you to get used to the feel texture and smell of this life-supporting product. It will enable you to become better at recognizing what healthy soil should look like, and you will soon reach a point where you can identify soil deficiencies almost instinctively. It really is the life force behind all gardening endeavours.

CONCLUSION

When you first started to consider the concept of growing vegetables in raised beds, the idea may have seemed a little counter-intuitive. We have, after all, been growing our crops directly in the ground since time immemorial. I hope now that you have been persuaded that this technique is not only practical but that it also offers many advantages.

In many ways, it differs little from more traditional methods of growing vegetables except that it takes some of the backaches out of work and allows for greater control of the growing medium. We might not have reached a point where this system is practical on a large-scale commercial basis. Still, for the small producer, particularly one with limited space available, it offers many plusses.

One added advantage is that raised beds can, when well designed, be aesthetically pleasing. While the large-scale farmer probably doesn't really care about this, if you are living in an urban environment, then why not have the benefits of something that pleases the eye as well as stocks the larder. Your neighbours will probably appreciate it too.

Raised beds can produce almost all of the crops that can be grown in the ground and often with better yields. The beds themselves can be as complicated or as simple as you the gardener chooses to make them. I suspect that if you follow a similar path to the one that I did, your designs and use of materials will develop as you gain in both confidence and experience. The same thing applies to your choice of plants. In the first book in this series, we stuck to those plants that are most commonly consumed. In this book, we have taken a more comprehensive look at vegetables and fruit, but we have still to scratch the tip of the iceberg. A gardener only needs to glance through a plant catalogue to understand that the pallet of vegetables we are accustomed to eating is minute when compared to what is out there. More and more frequently, we are offered seeds from Asia, Africa and South America, and they are opening up a whole new range of products for us to grow and eat.

Above all, I have tried to convey my belief that we can garden sustainably without seeing massive drops in yield due to pests or nutrient deficiencies. The organic movement is starting to gather momentum. At this stage, we have still to see that spreading into the more massive corporate farming arena, but it is undeniably happening among small producers. They are being rewarded by a buying public keen to purchase food that they know is both healthy for their families and sustainable for the planet. If you are starting to ride this wave, then I believe that your timing is right because it is a trend that is showing no sign of diminishing.

The emphasis of the first two books in this series, and those to follow, will always be on sustainability simply because I believe that all of the evidence points towards its importance, not just in the long term but also in the years that lie just ahead. Once the bug for growing your own food bites, then you will soon want to be sure that what you are offering your family and friends is of the best quality possible. If it is contaminated by chemicals you don't really understand, then you will always wonder if what you produce is healthy. There have been so many scandals related to the big agrochemical companies in recent years that it is difficult to distinguish fact from fiction. All I do know is that if I pay the proper attention to my soil, then I don't need them. I can produce healthy, chemical-free, environmentally friendly vegetables without needing to trust what it says on the side of a bottle of pesticide or bag of fertilizer. What is more, now that you have read this book, so can you.

Throughout this series of books, you will see that sustainability lies at the heart of all my gardening techniques. I make no apology for that. You will also discover that nearly all of the techniques link into each other at some point. That is not through some master plan on my part. It is derived from the fact that gardening is a natural and integrated process and many of the subjects overlap and build on one another. In the next book on companion planting, you will see that soil quality and choice of plants remains as crucial as it was in the first two books.

Thank you for reading my book. If you have enjoyed reading it perhaps you would like to leave a star rating and a review for me on Amazon? It really helps support writers like myself create more books. You can leave a review for me by scanning the QR code below:

Thank you so much.

Peter Shepperd